Fate Finally Found Us
Tommy and Barbara Beal: A Compelling Story of Rock 'n' Roll, His Overcoming Addiction, and Rediscovering Love
Barb Beal

Copyright © 2024 shared by Barbara Beal

All rights reserved.

No portion of this book may be reproduced in any form without written permission from the publisher or author except as permitted by U.S. copyright law.

This book is borne from a tapestry of memories, woven together with the support and warmth of friends and family who have illuminated our past with laughter and joy. A heartfelt gratitude to John H. Tate, whose dedication and expert touch in writing have been indispensable—without him, these pages would remain unwritten. We are also deeply thankful to Roger Murrah for connecting us with Michelle Robinson (Halverson) and her remarkable team of writers, whose talents have beautifully shaped this narrative.

May you, the reader, find as much joy in these stories as we found in recounting them. Above all, we acknowledge the grace of God and the thousands of angels who have guarded us in our most challenging moments. And to Tommy, who sparred with me, challenging each memory and detail—this journey through our shared past could not have been as rich without your fierce spirit.

Contents

1. A Love Story   1
2. Forever Bonded but Not Yet Ready   19
3. My Life Away from Tommy   27
4. Tommy's Adventures in the Sky and Beyond   33
5. Tommy's LOVE of Music!   53
6. Secrets of the Rock Star Diaries and More   63
7. Fate Finally Found Its Way To Us   96

1
A Love Story

MANY OF US HAVE been in love at one time or another in our lives. We've reminisced with friends about our first kiss, our first date, the butterflies we felt in the pit of our stomach when someone swooped in and captured our heart. As a culture I think we are just in love with the idea of love itself. Most meet and fall in love young, high school, college, we are still at ages where we are willing to jump in with both feet and give love a try. Then there are those rare couples you meet who have had a life time of love. They met when they were kids, fell in love and spent their lives pouring into one another, best friends, lovers, parents, and eventually grandparents.

My story, our story, is neither of those. In fact, it took a life time for us to find our true love. I believe our beautiful love story will captivate your heart and lift your soul. It's mixed with some adventure, some life challenges, and a lot of fate. God has a way of directing our lives even when we don't know he is doing so. We've heard the line many times in love stories, "finding my way back to you". Well, my (Barbara) story, Tommy's story, is about two people who throughout life kept finding their way back to one another.

Let me start with a little bit of background on the two of us.

History in the Making!

I (Barbara) was born in the Spring of 1950 on O'Shaunessy Avenue in Huntsville Alabama, to John Berton; (people called him JB) and Rubie Jacks. My mom wanted to name me Cheryl, however, my dad won out and they named me Barbara Ann Jacks. Daddy was a carpenter; he later became the head of the Carpenter's Union.

My mother was a stay-at-home homemaker until I was about fourteen years old. One of her unique special gifts was sewing. She loved it and it would be what would land her the job in the alterations department of the Loveman's Department Store located in "The Mall." Funny thing the actual name of the mall was "The Mall." It had opened in 1966 when malls were becoming a thing of the times. She worked at the Mall, and my dad used his unique gifts to help actually build it. He was the foreman who helped to oversee the building of The Mall. I remember sitting around the table with some of the guys they had sent down from New York City to help build it. They just loved my mom's pinto beans and cornbread. We had a loving family with a lot of care for people and life. I am thankful for it, especially all these years later. I have so many beautiful memories of my growing up.

My brother Donald was two years older than me, my brother

Clark was one year younger, and my brother Steve was two years younger than me. I'll never forget the day I found out mom was expecting again. I was just sure I was going to get a baby sister. With three brothers I longed to have a sister. Someone to play with dolls with me, and do all the other fun stuff girls do. It seemed like it took forever for the baby to be born, at least it seemed like it in my young mind. But at last, the big day came; Mama had to go to the hospital. I could barely stand the anticipation.

Daddy drove Mama to the hospital that day and instead of coming back with my new little sister to my disappointment he had other news. Trying to make it as exciting and as memorable as possible he lifted me up off the ground with his big strong arms and with a big smile on his face and said, "You have a new baby brother, and his name is Thomas!"

I felt so disappointed in the news. What? Another brother? How could this be? I was sure I was going to have a new baby sister. I had dreamed about us playing together, exchanging secrets and finally having someone who would want to do things with me! I cried and begged Daddy for a baby sister. Why couldn't they just exchange Thomas for a girl?

The next day we received the most devastating news. Little Thomas had died in the hospital of Hyaline Membrane disease (HMD), also called respiratory distress syndrome (RDS) which is a condition causing babies to need oxygen and help with their breathing. It's a common illness in babies and if it would happened today they may have been able to save him with all the technology that has come along in the past thirty plus years.

Thomas never came home and in my little five-year old mind I blamed myself. I didn't want another brother so somehow maybe God decided to take him away. Of course, this is far from the truth, but it's how I felt at the time. We were all so heart broken.

It would be only a year later when we'd find out mom was expecting again. My little brother Larry was born in the Spring of 1957. Mom brought him home on my birthday; I was seven years old. I didn't say one word about not having a sister. I was just grateful Larry came home. While I didn't say anything, mom knew. She knew how desperately I had wanted a little sister. In an effort to ease some of my disappointment, she told me Larry was gonna be my baby and I could feed and take care of him. Well, she was a wise woman. Not only did it make me feel a deeper connection to him, it also helped her tremendously.

Later that same year we moved from Huntsville to Toney Alabama. This was the very first house that had a bathroom inside the house. Yep! I spent most of my elementary years with an outhouse having to go outside in the freezing cold, and in the heat of summer was not fun. Not to mention they smelled horrible. Some of you reading this may not remember outhouses. The closest thing to it today would be the porta johns you see on construction sites, or at events but even those are nicer than the out-house we grew up with some of my childhood.

Before we had the bathroom, I was petrified of going to the bathroom. You never knew if you'd find a snake on the way there or even inside, and I never went once it got dark. It was a huge deal for our family and not only did we get the inside bathroom, it came with what felt like at the time, a huge bathtub. I was so little it felt like it was big enough to swim in. Seriously.

Toney was only about 14.5 miles Northwest of Huntsville and 10 miles Southwest of Hazel Green. Yet my world did change. We moved across the street from my mom's parents the Clarks; I called them Granny and Granddaddy. It was so nice having them close by.

Cotton was king in the South especially from the early 1920s through the 1960s and Huntsville was the also the watercress capital of the world. However, a new industry was emerging in the Huntsville area and it would put our tucked away little city on the global forefront giving our community a real leading edge. Redstone Arsenal, an army base, located outside of Huntsville, produced rockets and military explosives at the time. This opened the door for *The Space Program* being launched. There was a migration of German engineers to Huntsville after World War Two and in 1950 Dr. Werner von Braun a German rocket scientist brought his team of scientists to Huntsville. Redstone Arsenal, developed the Redstone Rocket and the Jupiter-C Rocket. Explorer 1, America's first orbiting satellite, launched on January 31, 1958, on top of the Jupiter-C Rocket. This was such a huge deal to our little unassuming community.

Dr. Von Braun, and his team, also helped to create a technology research area in Huntsville, which was known at the time as the second-largest research park in the United States. The U.S. Space & Rocket Center is also located here along with the US Space Camp. In the sixties, Huntsville AL became known as "The Rocket City," and "The Space Capital" because of its leading role in space exploration. NASA's Marshall Space Flight Center is also based here.

My dad, was one of the leading skilled carpenters in our area and had the privilege of working on the construction of several buildings on Redstone Arsenal. He also got to meet Warner Von Braun, one of the leading figures of rocket technology and said he was a really nice guy. My Uncle Charles, Dad's brother, worked for the Marshall Space Flight Center until he retired. Not sure what year he retired but it was in the late 70s or early 80s. The space center and all it brought with it to Huntsville, changed the trajectory of the city forever.

Dad rose up the ranks in his profession eventually teaching at the Huntsville Center and becoming the President of the Carpenters Union. Dad's health was declining and at 39 years young he would experience his first heart attack. It was 1967. I will never forget it. We were all so concerned over him but nothing stopped him. January 22, 1974, at the age of 45, in Decatur, Alabama, Dad died doing what he loved. He died of a massive heart attack standing at a podium telling a joke about getting old. Yep, that was my dad. Always using humor to connect and love people.

Those young years growing up I was fascinated by my dad and his ability to work with wood. He could build almost anything. In our home we had only two bedrooms; so, when I was about ten years old my dad built a bedroom just for me. I am sure I showed him my love and appreciation but I am not quite sure I ever told him just how special I thought he was. One of those things you look back on and wish you might have said or done just a little bit more.

Dad rose up the ranks in his profession eventually teaching at the Huntsville Center and becoming the President of the Carpenters Union. Dad's health was declining and at 39 years young he would experience his first heart attack. It was 1967. I will never forget it. We were all so concerned over him but nothing stopped him. January 22, 1974, at the age of 45, in Decatur, Alabama, Dad died doing what he loved. He died of a massive heart attack standing at a podium telling a joke about getting old. Yep, that was my dad. Always using humor to connect and love people.

After dad died we moved across the street from my mom's parents the Clarks; I called them Granny and Granddaddy so she could have some help continuing to raise us.

Tommy's Beginnings

Tommy was born in December, just ten months after his parents married on Valentine's Day. In those days most people didn't waste time waiting to start a family. There weren't as concerned about having the finances or a big enough home. Our home was by today's standards not considered big enough for our family and yet it was perfect.

Tommy's family lived on Vanderbilt Circle in Huntsville, Alabama. Tommy's dad worked for Thiokol Corporation on Redstone Arsenal. They manufactured missiles until it closed in 1996. Tommy's mom was a bookkeeper at Genesco Shoe Plant in Lowe Mill. Life was great for a time on Vanderbilt Circle but life took a turn. No one is ever prepared for major life changes. They just happen upon us and it happened to the Beal family. Tommy's dad was killed in an explosion at Thiokol that also killed three other men.

The family was devastated. After his dad's death, Tommy kept having nightmares. He would awaken in the night with his heart beating and an overwhelming feeling of sadness. Memories of his dad were everywhere. Eventually his mom realized something needed to change and she decided to move them to Toney to live with her parents. Being a single mom was challenging for her. Tommy and his mom went to the cemetery daily for over a year. There was a bench in the cemetery his mom would go and sit on recounting the memories and processing his death. Tommy would do the same, holding a conversation with his dad and hoping and believing he could hear him.

Thankfully Tommy was extremely close to his grandfather, who he called Dad; and his grandmother (granny). All Tommy had to do was mention something he wanted, and someone would get it for him: Dad, granny, or his Aunt Evelyn. Tommy never rode the school bus with us. His mom was very protective of him and took him in the morning, and Dad (his grandfather) picked him up in the afternoon. Our bus passed by Tommy's house every day. He would wait till I got off the bus and ride his bike or scooter down excited to see me. We would always invite him for dinner o those days and he would often accept our invite. Mom just loved when he'd come to dinner because he was so expressive at how much he just loved her cooking. There could never be too many people at our dinner table and secretly I was thrilled anytime he would stay.

His childhood while difficult because of the loss of his dad, he never lacked for anything. There was a lot of love and to a big degree he pretty much got anything he could ever want. He does remember just one incident he didn't get what he wanted. He is laughing as he shares this story with me. He had gone on a special trip to Florida with his Aunt Evelyn. The drive became a little monotonous so she pulled off the highway and the store they went into was selling a monkey. Yep, you heard me right. They were selling a monkey.

Tommy really wanted one of this monkey. Aunt Evelyn must not have had the heart to tell him no so she told him they'd pick the monkey up on the way back. His mother wasn't having it. She put her foot down on this one and Tommy came home from the trip empty handed or should I say empty monkey handed (laughing).

Tommy had a special relationship with the man he now called Dad, his grandfather. He had such a large booming voice and it would scare me. If he told me Barbara come here sis, you better believe I would move fast to get there. The entire family would attend church every Sunday. If Tommy talked in church, Dad would pull his ears, a sign to let him know he better be quiet. Afer church he couldn't wait to get home to eat Granny's cooking. She always cooked a huge meal on Sundays for the entire family and I always loved when I could be there for it. Cousins, Aunts, uncles, were all invited. Tommy and his cousin James ate till they were stuffed and then would go out and play football or baseball with the neighborhood kids. These were simpler times, good times.

Tommy says I was his best friend from the time we met. Our bond was strong from day one. I can't tell you why or explain it. It just existed. He confided in me about almost everything. One time he was dating a friend of mine and he was having problems with her, he asked me for advice. It was hard for me because I secretly held a deeper love for him in my heart, one it would take years to express. He would always tell me I was his best friend and I think he knew I would always be there for him.

We would go for walks, swing on the porch, and take long walks in the woods in the winter. He'd ride me on his bike, his scooter and his motorcycle. As we grew older we'd go get a burger together or some ice cream. It was never a date. Just time with my best friend. I think fate was always trying to tell us something but we just didn't see it, or at least we didn't want to see it for what it really was. Even after we had all moved out of that house and back to Huntsville, Tommy would go and sit in our driveway and talk to me in his mind. Even when that house burned down the driveway still left in tact, he would keep going and sitting in it, thinking of me.

We drifted away over time from each other but what we never knew is we were always close by. When I was living in Atlanta he was, only a mile apart but neither of us knew that at the time. I was living in Germany when he was living in Belgium, only a few hours away. I then moved to San Antonio and he was living in Houston. What's crazy is we never knew it until years later when we reconnected.

The Luck of Tommy Beal

Throughout his life, Tommy Beal has survived some close calls, and he has seemingly walked into some great opportunities. As outside observers, many would say that Tommy was very lucky. Being a man of faith, he would correct everyone and simply say that he has been blessed, not lucky. However, so that all readers will understand, and grasp the point, I will highlight what some would call The Luck of Tommy Beal.

Tommy's Dad's Funeral

By no means would anyone suggest that the death of Tommy's dad, when he was only four years old, was lucky or even a good thing. The tragedy that took Tommy's dad's life, along with three other men, could have destroyed his family. However, this tragedy in Tommy's life did not end him. He became stronger after each challenge he faced in life. Tommy has always had faith, he went to church every Sunday growing up. We all went to church together.

Tommy, his granddad (dad) and his cousin James Taylor.

Many times church was just another social event for him to be with all his friends. His grandfather played a very important role in his going to church, fostering his strong belief in God, and knowing God was in control of everything, even when he was flying.

In Toney, Tommy's life was what many kids could only dream of. For example, on the farm, Tommy had a horse named Dixie, a brown and white quarter horse filly. Dixie was bought for Tommy by his mother.

Tommy at age 7 with his horse Dixie

He also had a donkey named Pete, which was bought for him by his granddad. This happened when he was only seven years old.

Down the road from Tommy's grandparent's farm was a man named Mr. Goode. He also had a donkey, and he would hitch his donkey to a wagon and take Tommy for rides. Tommy looked forward to the rides with Mr. Goode because of the talks they would have. As Tommy reflects on those days, he recalls, "Most of the men in our neighborhood took time with me because they all knew the history of my father's death."

At such a young age, Tommy may not have considered how

fortunate he was to live such a wonderful life. After all, it was just the way things were for him at the time. On that fateful day when Tommy got on his American Flyer bicycle and headed off to the McCutcheon's Grocery Store, my older brother Donald and I were walking to McCutcheon's to exchange Coke bottles for candy. When I saw Tommy, he was riding the bike like he was gliding in the clouds. I was seven years old at the time, and Tommy was nine.

Tommy rode over to us and introduced himself; there was an instant attraction for both of us. He offered me a ride on the back of his bike, and I gladly accepted. It would be unfair to say that it was Tommy's luck alone that brought us together that day. However, I will concede that Tommy's luck played a major role in us becoming lifelong friends.

After that day, Tommy would ride to my house several times a week to sit and talk. We would ride his bike or just walk around and talk about everything that was happening at the time. It was during our talks that Tommy revealed that he wanted to fly. However, it was sometime later before he explained to me why flying was so important to him. He said, "If I could fly, I would be up in the clouds and closer to my dad."

At age ten, Tommy got a Cushman scooter. As his best friend, I was the first person to whom he gave a ride. That scooter got him into so much trouble. Once, he snuck off on his scooter to go swimming with a bunch of area friends. They went to what we called the Blue Hole, it was on Wall Triana. The water was deep, and his mom was terrified of water and told him he couldn't go, but he snuck off anyway. She found him, even though he said he was trying to go underwater so she wouldn't see him. She took his scooter away, and he was grounded for a week. He tried to ride his bike, but the tires had rotted since it had sat up so long without being ridden.

Tommy at age 10 with his Cushman.

At eleven years old, Tommy rode horses in a Fox Hunt at Harry Rhett's place with one of our neighbors Colonel Horner. His grandmother made his outfit and found him a riding cap (we still have the hat). Tommy & I spent a lot of time at the Colonel's house riding and learning to jump with his horses.

We kids never thought about Harry Rhett or why he seemed to have so many resources. As we grew older, his community influences were more evident. A quick Google search of his name, one would find that Harry Rhett was "Chairman of the Huntsville Waterworks Utility Board and the Huntsville Gas Utility Board. He had been a Major in the United States Army. As it relates to horses, he was a member of the Masters of Foxhound Association, The National Steeplechase, and the Hunt Association of Maryland. On top of that, he was the president of the Huntsville-Madison County Chamber of Commerce. People would not have thought that he was also a member of the Harvard Club of New York City. Locally he was a member of the Byrd Spring Rod and Gun Club and president of the Huntsville Rotary Club.

As for Colonel Horner, I am not sure if any of us ever knew his true story. I did learn later in life that he was a decorated officer in the United States Army. This was the kind of lifestyle Tommy lived as a child, and his friends, especially me, all benefited too. If such influential friends surround you, from such an early life, is it possible to take stock and realize how lucky or blessed you are? Or do you see it as this is just the way things are?

Dot, Tommy's mother, worked as a Bookkeeper for General Shoe before Edwin's death. At one time, Huntsville city proper was segmented into districts based on various textile production. General Shoe (later named Genesco) manufactured army boots and was located in the Low Mill district.

Although Tommy enjoyed being in the band, playing sports,

and riding motorbikes, his passion was flying. Tommy told everyone he wanted to fly for as long as I can remember. As a young boy, he would watch planes fly over his house and watch the crop dusters. Tommy would stand, watch the planes fly overhead, and fall over watching them. His grandmother would say, "Honey, just sit down and watch them." If he were at my house, he would talk on and on about flying planes, he never wanted to do anything else.

Our friend Mac McCutcheon who was 3 years younger than Tommy, said one of his earliest memories was of Tommy and Ray Lassiter standing outside the church with their jeans cuffed, which was a fad then. Cuffed blue jeans with white socks and loafers. He thought that was the coolest thing ever. Mac's dad and Tommy's mom dated for a long time and almost got married, but Tommy's grandma didn't like the idea of him being a divorced man with a child. It was Mac's grandparents who owned the McCutcheon Grocery store.

Mac recounts a time when his dad and Dot were going to the Drive-In Theater. Mac went with them and was supposed to go to sleep but stayed awake the entire time. Later his mom married Jimmy Giles.

One might have thought that two best friends' parents dating would be strange; however, Mac and Tommy were close and were even looking forward to being brothers. Although the parents never married, Tommy and Mac were very close, and are still close all these years later.

2

Forever Bonded but Not Yet Ready

How is it possible at the young age of just seven years old, you can meet someone and they have a profound impact on your life from the moment you meet them? They leave an imprint on your heart that remains etched inside of your soul forever. Tommy Beal literally had me at hello. He was always in my rear view mirror no matter where I was in life, but I had to keep my eyes on the road ahead and it would be years later before he would go from being in the rear-view mirror to right in front of me.

I'll never forget the first time I saw him. My older brother Donald and I had decided to walk to McCutcheon's Grocery Store, only a mile down the road from our home, to exchange Coke bottles for candy. That's what we did back in my day. Our days were met with excitement when we could go get candy. It was such a treasure to find coke bottles, which at the time were only in glass and could be exchanged for money or for candy so the Coca Cola company could recycle the bottles.

There he was riding his American Flyer bicycle, arms outstretched, his wavy brown tousled hair blowing in the wind.

It's funny how we see things at a young age. He was just a kid riding his bike down the street but in my adolescent mind, it was as if he was a majestic prince riding right to me, his princess. It's a memory so vivid in my mind to this day.

My life truly would change that day, but little did I know the impact it would have on my life forever. Tommy and I would build a life-long friendship, one I so longed and desired to become more. Yet it would be years before that dream would be realized. This is our story. Two people, two lives, to different journeys yet always inter-woven in my mind.

Around people I didn't know I was a little shy, but if I knew you and trusted you we could have fun. As Tommy and I grew up my trust in him grew stronger each year. Maybe it was all that time we spent with me riding on the back of his bicycle and later his scooter. A bond of trust was forged, and he never broke it. I always felt he would protect me.

Tommy came to the house at least once a week, sometimes more depending on what was happening. Anything significant in his life he always shared with me. My parents loved Tommy, so they never said anything about him coming over to the house so often and my dad really felt for Tommy because he had lost his father so young. It also helped that Tommy was always so courteous and respectful.

When we moved to Toney, our house was surrounded by woods. My brothers and I along with Tommy spent many hours in the woods building forts and tree houses. I was terrified of snakes so I would only go in the woods during the winter months. We loved building and hanging out in the tree houses. It was always so much fun feeling like we were in another world but getting down from those houses for me was always so scary. Not to mention I was also afraid of heights so my brothers Clark and Steve or Tommy would have to help me down. One time they actually left me up there because they grew tired and frustrated of helping me. Boys can be so mean at times. I laugh about it now but I was traumatized when they left me there. Thank God my mother made them come back and help me down or who knows, I might still be up there. (smile).

Also, Tommy loved his Cushman scooter; we would ride to the store around our yard or just sit on it talking. I so wanted to drive it but he never offered to teach me.

He ended up graduating to a Yamaha motorcycle and took a nasty fall burning his leg badly. After he was all bandaged up, he came right to my house to show me. We always ran to one another first when anything happened in our life, and as crazy as it sounds when one of us was hurt the other one would feel the pain.

We would talk for hours about our dreams, our hopes, our view of the world at the time. He knew early on he wanted to be a pilot. He loved everything about the idea of flying. I dreamed of being a nurse. I loved the idea of helping people and have a nurturing heart. I never did become a nurse, however, over my lifetime I have worked closely with the profession. I've held positions as a Ward Secretary, a Red Cross Volunteer, a Family Practice Doctor's Office Manager, a Billing Manager for a doctor's office, and an Office Manager for a Surgeon's office. When I retired, I was the Business Manager for an Internal Medicine Group.

It's funny how you can spend countless hours with a boy and only be seen as their best friend. As the years moved on, I never sensed Tommy wanting or desiring me in any way other than his best friend. We were so close, but in my heart he felt far. If I were dating someone he didn't trust he'd tell me, and I did the same with him. As best friends and shared everything about our ongoing dating life. He'd come back from a date and tell me what they did; well, not everything, some things were off-limits of course (smile).

I begin to see a pattern with him. Tommy would date a girl till the excitement wore off and then he was on to the next one, always looking for something new and exciting. Never able to commit. Some years later he told me that what he was looking for was right in front of him, but he couldn't slow down long enough to realize it. I kind of knew he felt that way a little bit but by the time he actually said it to me, the years had grown up between us and I didn't feel at the time I could really trust in what he was telling me. Then something would happen that would change everything between us. Another man came into the picture.

When Don came along, I was just tired of waiting on Tommy Beal. Do you blame me? We had been friends since we were in elementary school and he still didn't see me. I met Don in high school. It was beautiful fall day, the air was crisp and the energy from the county fair was electrifying. Don had been dating my friend Patsy, and had asked her to go to the fair, but she couldn't go. It's amazing how one incident can change the trajectory of your life. Patsy called me and asked me to go with him instead.

Don and I went to the fair; I thought he was charming initially and we had such a great time. He must have felt the same because he immediately broke up with Patsy and he and I started dating.

Don was fun to be around, he had a great sense of humor. He always paid a lot of attention to me, something I had longed for from Tommy. It felt good to have someone care about me and pursue me.

My friendship with Patsy ended for obvious reasons and it wouldn't be restored until we hit our fifties. I reached out to her on Facebook. It was a little scary since I did not know how she would respond. I had no clue if she would talk to me or even remember me. She did respond and it turned out she was happily married and had a great life.

I remember when I finally decided to tell Tommy I was going to marry Don. He didn't like Don because he'd heard negative things about him and his family. He was very upset and tried to get me not to marry him. He asked me to wait and see how things would go with us. But I knew that Tommy and I wanted different things and we were going in different directions. I went ahead and married Don, but in my heart I never stopped loving Tommy.

Over time I learned about the life Tommy lived while we were apart and his first wife. In Atlanta, Tommy found that he enjoyed strip clubs, and he would go to them frequently. Once he moved to Maryland from Atlanta, he inquired about local strip clubs and one of his coworkers suggested Johnny's, a club that had beautiful exotic dancers.

To hear Tommy tell it, "I was not disappointed in what I saw, and I was there several times a week. I was there so often that I became friends with Johnny the owner. The thing is I didn't go home every weekend, so I spent a lot of money and time at Johnny's. Johnny and I became such friends that when he got married, he asked me to be a bartender at his wedding."

Little did Tommy know that his life was about to take a little change at the wedding. One of the girls at the club, Deborah, had attracted Tommy's attention. She was petite blonde and cute. Tommy said she reminded him of me, you know cute, petite, and cute ha-ha. Deborah was also at that wedding. Tommy remembers, "Johnny knew I was interested in Deborah so as a little surprise he introduced me to her at the wedding. What an introduction, Deborah and I became fast friends, and we spent all our free time together."

People would ask Tommy if it ever bothered him that Deborah was a dancer. "No, that never bothered me." He said "And once we became a couple, she gave up that way of life. She changed her life to be with me; no telling how many men offered to take her away from that life. I just considered myself lucky with all the guys she was around and some of them better looking than I was, but it was me who flew in and swept her away."

Deborah accompanied Tommy to one of the air shows. While flying she was painting her toenails and told Tommy he had better not make her spill the polish. In the Tommy Beal tradition, he proceeded to do a barrel roll and did not spill a drop. "I enjoyed showing out for her and she loved the attention."

In 1984 Tommy accepted a job selling planes for Mitsubishi. He and Deborah moved to Houston TX and entered into a common law marriage, beginning their lives as a married couple. Deborah also worked as a flight attendant for Tommy on his plane.

Tommy seemed to have everything he wanted in his wife, she was a free-spirit Flight Attendant on his plane and good-looking too. When asked what happened? Tommy said, "I just got tired of the way things were going between us. She was interested in other men, and I was partying way too much. On top of all of that, I was also homesick for Alabama. Deborah wasn't interested in leaving Houston at that point. However, after we split up, she later moved to Tennessee moving in with her parents and sister."

Although they were in a common law marriage since Deborah used his last name when they bought a house and in other legal matters in Texas they had to get a legal divorce.

3
My Life Away from Tommy

Don and I got married at his parents' house, a modest home nestled in a quiet neighborhood. It was a sunny afternoon, the kind where the air feels warm and full of promise. I remember feeling a mix of excitement and dread as I walked down the makeshift aisle, the scent of freshly mown grass and blooming gardenias in the air.

From the very start, my marriage to Don was rocky. We argued over the smallest things, and the love I had hoped would grow never did. Things only got worse after he joined the Air Force. The constant moving, the long absences, and the strain of military life took their toll on us.

I realized what Tommy and I had were totally different. We were close ever since, our childhoods intertwined with laughter and shared dreams. We talked a few times after I got married, but as the years passed, our conversations became less frequent. His dream of becoming a pilot was realized and he worked hard to achieve his goals. I only hear about him every time my mom would occasionally give me updates when he was in town. Every time she mentioned his name, a wave of bittersweet nostalgia washed over me, bringing back memories of our simpler days which I wished I still had during my marriage.

I can vividly recall how every time I flew into or out of an airport, my heart would skip a beat as I watched the pilots walking through the terminals. I was always looking for him, hoping for a glimpse of Tommy. I'd reflect on our childhood, and a sense of joy would fill my heart. It's like there's always something inside me that hopes that maybe at some point will cross paths again. It's a feeling that never left me. Even the pilot's announcement over the intercom would make my heart jump, only to sink again when I realized it wasn't my Tommy. It's strange to think how often we were in close proximity to each other, city-wise, yet our paths never crossed. But for me our hearts, I believe, were never far apart.

I still remembered clearly how my heart was heavy because my dad didn't come during my wedding. He thought I was making a mistake, yet for me, during that time it felt like it was the best decision I have ever made. Aren't we all hoping to marry the person we fell in love with? To walk down that aisle thinking that they will be the one who is going to be with us in this lifetime? The anticipation and happiness felt like a dream come true only to be awakened with the hard truth of reality where I realized that maybe my dad was right all along. Maybe it was indeed a mistake. This realization hit me when the bad ones started to outweigh the good ones we have together. My marriage to Don was filled with more bad times than good. Looking back I can say that the ceremony and what we shared itself is a blur now, a hazy memory of vows and smiles that didn't quite reach the eyes, or even a lifetime.

Realizing these makes me wonder what drew me to Don. Was it his dark hair, styled just like Tommy's, or his similar personality? Looking back, I realize that I might have seen him as a way to hold on to a part of Tommy, but I was wrong. My marriage to Don was nothing like what I had with Tommy.

However, it is a part of me that will never be removed no matter how hard I try to forget, partly it helped me to know clearly what I really want and to let go of things that I thought will be mine forever. Despite all the unhappiness, these situations brought two bright lights in my life: my daughters, Sherry and Donna. Sherry, with her curious mind and gentle nature, and Donna, with her boundless energy and fierce determination.

Sherry, my oldest, was always the studious one. She loved to read and had a natural curiosity about the world. Donna, two years younger, was my little athlete. She threw herself into gymnastics with a passion that took her to regionals in Texas. When she grew tired of the repetition, she turned to swimming and then to dance roller skating, winning awards and making me proud at every turn. Today, they both live in Alabama, successful and happy in their own ways. They were my parachute, the reason I kept going when I thought I couldn't survive the fall I had to take during that time. We tried as much as possible to focus on the good things and put behind us the things that's never pretty but necessary for us to realize and appreciate the good things that were left in that marriage.

My girls were my life. Everything I did, I did with them in mind...even staying with Don . They were close growing up, although they drifted apart as they got older. We went through a lot of hard times, but we made it through together. When we were stationed in Japan, they joined the Girl Scouts, and we often hosted Japanese girls for cultural exchange events. Those were some of the happiest times, filled with laughter and learning.

For the most part, it was just the girls and me. Don was an absentee father, partly due to his Air Force duties and partly by choice. He came from a very dysfunctional family and didn't realize the impact of his behavior until much later, when the girls were grown. Despite his absence, my daughters thrived. Sherry pursued a career with determination, and Donna excelled in sports, dance, and everything she set her mind to.

I realize that my life has been a series of ups and downs, but the love of my daughters and the joy of my grandchildren and great-grandchildren have made it all worthwhile. Each day is a blessing, and I am thankful for the journey that has brought me to where I am today.

I often find myself lost in memories of the past, thinking about the paths I took and the ones I didn't. There are moments of regret, but also moments of immense gratitude. The scent of gardenias still takes me back to that sunny afternoon when I married Don, and the sound of a plane overhead still makes my heart skip a beat, thinking of Tommy.

Throughout my life, I have felt God's presence. In my darkest moments, I have felt His arms around me, giving me strength to carry on. I have heard His words and seen His work in my life. He has blessed me in countless ways, and it serves no purpose to dwell on the negative parts of my marriage. I am still grateful for the second chance I got, and more on that later. I truly believe He led Tommy and I back together, and if we had been paying attention, it might have happened sooner.

I hope to share not just the story of my life, but the lessons I've learned along the way. Life is indeed full of unexpected turns, isn't it? And while some may lead to heartache, others lead to joy and fulfillment. What I learned from that marriage is that the key is to keep moving forward, to cherish the good times, and to learn from the bad.

I believe what happened is God's way of reminding me I am never alone, there is always hope. This faith has carried me through the toughest moments, giving me strength and guiding me toward better days.

Sherry and Donna are now mothers themselves, raising their children with the same love and care I tried to give them. Watching them grow into such strong, capable women fills me with pride. They have their own struggles, their own triumphs, but I know they will always have each other, just as I have always had them.

Reflecting on my journey, I am reminded of a quote I once read:

"Life is not measured by the number of breaths we take, but by the moments that take our breath away." There have been many such moments in my life, both good and bad, and they have shaped me into the person I am today.

I am currently filled with a deep sense of peace and amazement on how everything works out for good. My life may not have turned out the way I once imagined, but it has been rich with experiences, lessons, and love. I have been blessed in so many ways, and for that, I am eternally grateful.

Life is indeed a journey that is full of unexpected twists and turns. We must embrace each moment, cherish the ones you love, and never lose sight of the blessings that surround you. And remember, no matter how dark the night may seem, the dawn always brings a new day, filled with hope and endless possibilities.

That was my life back then. It was a life I thought I wanted and felt sure about in the beginning, but what I realized is that it takes two people to make a marriage grow and have love. While my marriage ended, what I realized is yes it was a loss, but it was also a beginning of reclaiming my story—a chance to create a new chapter where my dreams weren't grounded and caged. I had life again and a new reality where my spirit could soar and take flight once again.

4

Tommy's Adventures in the Sky and Beyond

Flying Lessons at Fourteen

Tommy was always a boy of many passions. He loved being in the band, playing sports, and riding motorbikes, but none of these could match his true passion: flying. For as long as I can remember, he would tell everyone he met that he wanted to fly. As a young boy, he would gaze up at the sky, mesmerized by the planes soaring overhead, and stand in awe watching the crop dusters at work. His eyes lit up with wonder every time a plane flew by, and his grandmother often had to remind him, "Honey, just sit down and watch them," worried he might fall over from staring too hard.

Whenever Tommy was at my house, he could talk endlessly about airplanes. His enthusiasm was contagious, and it was clear he never wanted to do anything else. His dream began to take shape when he was about 14. His stepdad, Jimmy Giles, recognizing Tommy's unwavering passion, took him to Huntsville Aviation and helped him land a job washing and fueling airplanes. This was Tommy's paradise, and he was thrilled to be around the planes he adored.

Tommy started taking flying lessons as soon as he was old enough. Mr. Watley, the President of Huntsville Aviation, played a crucial role in Tommy's journey, helping him get started with his lessons. Tommy often came to my house excitedly to share tales of his flying adventures. He would describe in detail the thrill of keeping the plane level and maintaining altitude, his eyes sparkling as he recounted his maneuvers.

The day Tommy did his first solo flight was monumental. He was so elated that he came to get me, and we rushed back to the airport. There, he proudly showed me the plane he had flown solo in. Though I couldn't fly alone with him until he got his license at 17, I shared his joy and anticipation.

Tommy quickly became good friends with Frank Mickle, and they would often fly to Auburn together, with Tommy keen to build up his flight hours. Always supportive, Mr. Watley helped Tommy start selling airplanes to fund his flight lessons. Tommy's dedication was unwavering, and he worked various jobs, including a stint as a lifeguard at Blue Water Springs Park in Toney, Alabama. Naturally, he enjoyed the company of girls in their swimsuits, and he worked alongside one of our teachers, Mr. Farmer. I still chuckle, remembering Mr. Farmer telling me to stop trying to dive, fearing I might break my neck, a warning that Tommy found particularly amusing.

Tommy's family grew when his half-brother Donnie was

born just a month before Tommy's 16th birthday. To ensure Tommy didn't feel left out, his mom and stepdad gifted him a gold-colored 1965 Ford Falcon convertible as an early birthday present. Even before his license, Tommy couldn't wait to show me the car. I was the first person he took for a ride in it, and that Falcon became a symbol of many fun times and adventures, including sneaking friends into the fair by cramming them into the trunk to get in for free.

December 1965 when Tommy got his pilot license.

On his 17th birthday, December 1965, Tommy achieved his dream and got his pilot's license. It was a Monday, and we were off school for the Christmas holidays. The first thing Tommy did was come to call me so we could fly around together. He also took his mom and stepdad up, sharing his love of flying with those closest to him. Tommy's mom took us to celebrate at Shoney's Restaurant on the corner of Parkway and University Drive. It was the perfect end to a perfect day.

Shoney's Big Boy was the place to be for special occasions.

Opened in 1958 by Whorton and Julia Burgreen, it was the first with a unique architectural style known as "Hyperbolic Parabola." It had both inside seating and 50 drive-in stalls, making it the largest drive-in in the area until it was demolished in 1978. Many of its managers went on to open their own restaurants, making them a cornerstone of the community.

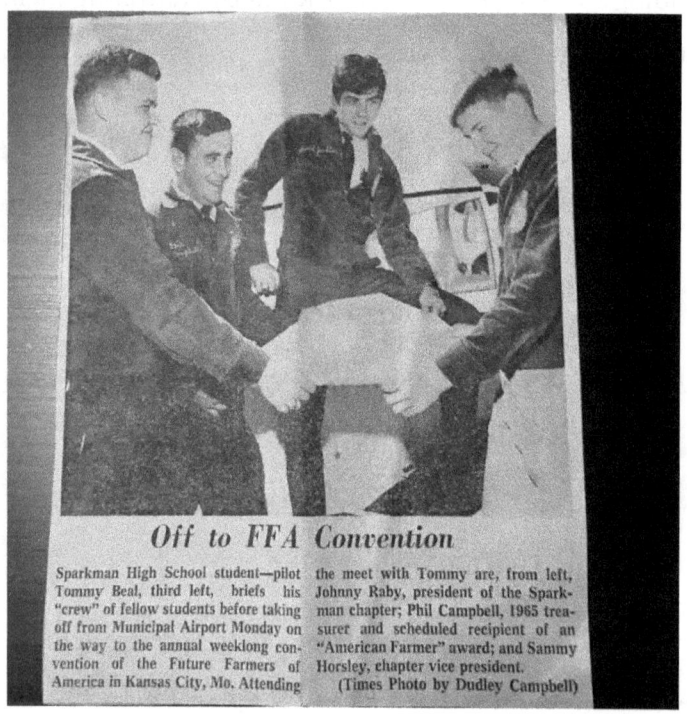

Off to FFA Convention

Sparkman High School student—pilot Tommy Beal, third left, briefs his "crew" of fellow students before taking off from Municipal Airport Monday on the way to the annual weeklong convention of the Future Farmers of America in Kansas City, Mo. Attending the meet with Tommy are, from left, Johnny Raby, president of the Sparkman chapter; Phil Campbell, 1963 treasurer and scheduled recipient of an "American Farmer" award; and Sammy Horsley, chapter vice president.

(Times Photo by Dudley Campbell)

With his license, Tommy continued to build his flight hours, even flying some classmates to Kansas City for a weeklong FAA conference. Parents trusted Tommy completely, knowing his skills and dedication. He took every opportunity to fly, often taking friends along. I remember how Greg and Johnny Allen were initially apprehensive about flying with Tommy. He reassured them, but in true Tommy fashion, he stopped the engine mid-flight to scare them. Greg later admitted it was terrifying, though Tommy knew exactly what he was doing.

Tommy's confidence in flying was unwavering. He even flew himself and his best friend, Danny Ray Robinson, to Montgomery to see Governor Lurleen Wallace's inauguration. There, they met a couple of blond and beautiful girls and enjoyed the inauguration and the after-party. Tommy always downplayed the details, but I knew he had a knack for adventure and charm.

Flying came naturally to Tommy, and his confidence in the cockpit was unmatched. This self-assurance permeated every aspect of his life, drawing people to him while sometimes pushing others away. Yet, through it all, I remained a constant presence, the first girl he took to the skies when he got his pilot's license, sharing his dreams and adventures.

Reflecting on those days, I see a boy whose passion and determination knew no bounds. Tommy's love for flying was more than a hobby; it was his life's calling. And in every flight and every story he shared, I felt privileged to be a part of his extraordinary journey.

Tommy Flying Charters

In 1967, Tommy went to the University of Alabama, and by 1969, he had graduated with an associate degree. It was a proud moment for him, but it also marked the beginning of a challenging chapter in his life. After graduation, Tommy moved to Atlanta to work for a major airline company. This period, however, wasn't something he liked to talk about much. The work was dull, and he couldn't come home as often as he wished. He felt trapped by the routine and longed for the freedom that flying charters and selling airplanes had once given him. His job mainly involved flying back and forth between Atlanta and Dallas, which quickly became monotonous.

During this time, Tommy dated many beautiful flight attendants. One, in particular, was a leggy blonde named Maria. Tommy described her as a pilot groupie, someone easy and fun to be around. They shared rooms and meals during layovers, but eventually, even this lost its charm. Tommy decided to return to charter flights and selling planes, yearning for the excitement and flexibility he had once enjoyed. Later in life, he sometimes regretted leaving the major airline because of the benefits he missed out on, but at the time, the thought never crossed his mind. He always referred to the company as the "major airline" without revealing its name.

In 1973, after leaving the major airline, one of Tommy's flight instructors, John Whitworth, got him a job flying for McKay Industries in Double Springs, Alabama. The first jet Tommy flew after leaving the major airline was the Citation. This sleek, fan jet had eight passenger seats, a bar and coffee rack, plush pilot seats, and a fully equipped instrument panel. Tommy loved flying it; the faster it went, the better. He flew for McKay

Industries for about a year before moving on to American Air Service in Gadsden, Alabama, which also operated charter flights.

At American Air Service, Tommy flew piston and turboprop charters and sold airplanes. The planes were cabin class, sometimes with a curtain or a wooden partition, and they had small bars and lavatories separating the pilots from the passengers. Tommy's main job was to fly business owners and their friends across several states. But he also had an unusual side job: flying dead bodies for funeral homes, especially for West Gadsden Funeral Home. He transported bodies to places like Illinois and New York.

The first time Tommy flew a body, he was freaked out. I remember him telling one of our neighbors about it. "The plane I was flying didn't have a co-pilot seat," he said, "so the dead body lay on a stretcher, with the head right next to me. That creeped me out a couple of times. Because of body gases and the turbulence, some of the bodies would pass gas. But the creepiest thing was when their eyes would open." Despite the initial nervousness, he got used to it after a while.

Tommy would explain, "They weren't in a casket, just on a gurney. We strapped them down so they wouldn't fall off if we hit rough weather. It was spooky at first, but okay after that." He always emphasized the importance of protecting the nose. "We put coat hangers over the corpse's head to keep from mashing the nose. The hanger would pull the sheet away from the nose, creating a guard over the face."

Talking about his time in Gadsden, Tommy shared, "My first live passenger was Tom Dawson, who owned Dawson Construction in Gadsden, Alabama. Tom Dawson's company later built a new jail in Huntsville, Alabama, though there was a lot of controversy due to the project's $50 million in cost overruns. Tom would always tell me, 'Never panic and that you're not dead till you take your last breath,' something I remembered each time I flew." Tommy spent about a year or two flying charter flights and ferrying businesspeople across the United States.

These were the days when Tommy's life was a mix of high-flying adventures and peculiar experiences. Looking back, it's clear that each flight, each journey, added a unique chapter to his story, shaping the confident and resilient person he became.

When Tommy was about 14, his stepdad, Mr. Giles, recognized his deep love for airplanes and decided to help him get closer to his dream. He took Tommy to Huntsville Aviation and helped him secure a job washing and fueling airplanes. Tommy was thrilled to be around planes, and he wasted no time in starting flying lessons as soon as he was old enough. Imagine the excitement of a young boy, barely a teenager, getting to be so close to the machines he adored.

Tommy was indeed fortunate to have a stepfather with the right contacts and resources to help him take those first steps into the world of aviation. But Tommy wasn't just lucky; he was also hardworking. He worked for Mr. Watley, the President of Huntsville Aviation, who played a crucial role in getting

Tommy started with his flying lessons. Tommy would often come over to my house, bubbling with excitement, to share his latest adventures in the sky. His eyes would light up as he talked about keeping the plane level while maintaining altitude and described some of his aerial maneuvers.

The day Tommy did his first solo flight was a day of immense pride and joy for him. He was so excited that he came to get me and took me back to the airport just to show me the plane he had flown solo. Though I couldn't fly alone with him until he got his license at 17, sharing that moment with him was special.

Tommy quickly made friends in the aviation community, like Frank Mickle, whom he flew to Auburn several times to build up his flight time. Mr. Watley, always supportive, also helped Tommy start selling airplanes, which allowed him to pay for his flight lessons. To make ends meet, Tommy even worked as a lifeguard at Blue Water Springs Park one summer in Toney, Alabama. He loved the job, not just for the money, but also for the chance to watch all the girls in their skimpy swimsuits. At seventeen, Tommy was already earning the nickname "Tommy the Blessed One," though he was still too humble to acknowledge it.

Even as a young pilot, Tommy had some fascinating experiences. One memorable trip was when he flew himself and his best friend, Danny Ray Robinson, to Montgomery to witness Governor Lurleen Wallace's inauguration. They took a taxi to the capital, where a couple of girls picked them up. Tommy can't remember much about the girls, except that they were blonde and beautiful. "We all went to the inauguration and the after-party. Danny and I had to leave the party to take a taxi to the airport; after all, I had to fly home," he would recall with a mischievous smile.

Governor Lurleen Wallace was the first woman governor of Alabama, inaugurated on January 16, 1967. She was married to George Wallace, who had served as governor before her but couldn't run for a third term due to state law. So, Lurleen ran and won, though it was no secret that George Wallace still held the reins of power.

Flying came so naturally to Tommy, and it filled him with a self-confidence that extended far beyond the cockpit. This confidence drew people to him and sometimes pushed them away. He didn't need to work at making friends; people were naturally drawn to him. Yet, in his youthful confidence, he might have overlooked some of the most important people in his life. I was the first girl he rode on his American Flyer bicycle, the first girl on the back of his motorbike, the first girl he took for a ride in his 1965 Ford Falcon, and yes, the first girl he took to the sky when he got his pilot's license. Our friendship remained strong, even if we never officially dated. Tommy later confessed that he wanted to ask me out but feared it might ruin our close friendship.

Tommy's life seemed charmed, guided by luck and the blessings he believed came from God. He felt God had saved him many times in risky situations, though he rarely shared these thoughts, living in a culture of partying where such beliefs weren't often voiced.

After high school, Tommy landed what many would consider a dream job with a major airline. He dated many beautiful flight attendants, including a memorable leggy blonde named Maria. "She was a pilot groupie," Tommy would say with a grin, "easy and fun to be around. On layovers, she and I would share a room and meals." Despite the perks, Tommy found airline flying monotonous, like driving a bus in the sky. He missed the joy and freedom of charter flights and selling planes. Looking back, he sometimes wished he had stuck with the airline for the benefits, but as a young man, that thought never crossed his mind.

In 1973, after leaving the airline, Tommy's flight instructor, John Whitworth, got him a job with McKay Industries in Double Springs, Alabama. The first jet Tommy flew there was the Citation, a sleek fan jet with eight passenger seats, a bar and coffee rack, plush pilot seats, and a fully equipped instrument panel. Tommy loved the speed and sophistication of the Citation. He flew for McKay Industries for about a year before moving on to American Air Service in Gadsden, Alabama, another charter service.

At American Air Service, Tommy flew piston and turboprop charters and sold airplanes. These planes were cabin class, sometimes divided by a curtain or wooden partition, with small bars and lavatories separating the pilots from the passengers. Tommy enjoyed flying business owners and their friends across several states.

Tommy also had an unusual job: flying dead bodies for funeral homes, especially West Gadsden Funeral Home. He transported bodies to places like Illinois and New York. The first time he flew a body, he was understandably freaked out. "The plane I was flying didn't have a co-pilot seat," he would tell me, "so the dead body lay on a stretcher, with the head right next to me. That creeped me out a couple of times. Because of body gases and the turbulence, some of the bodies would pass gas. But the creepiest thing was when their eyes would open." Over time, he got used to it, though it was always a bit unsettling.

Tommy would explain, "They weren't in a casket, just on a gurney. We strapped them down so they wouldn't fall off if we hit rough weather. It was spooky at first, but okay after that." He always made sure to protect the nose of the deceased. "We put coat hangers over the corpse's head to keep from mashing the nose. The hanger would pull the sheet away from the nose, creating a guard over the face."

Reflecting on his time in Gadsden, Tommy often spoke about his first live passenger, Tom Dawson, who owned Dawson Construction in Gadsden, Alabama. Dawson's company later built a new jail in Huntsville, Alabama, despite a lot of controversy over the project's $50 million cost overruns. Dawson had a saying that Tommy remembered every time he flew: "Never panic and that you're not dead till you take your last breath."

Tommy's life was a mix of high-flying adventures and peculiar experiences, each adding a unique chapter to his story. His confidence, charm, and passion for flying shaped his life and the lives of those around him. And through it all, I was there, the first girl he took to the skies, sharing in the thrill and wonder of his journey.

In 1974, Tommy packed his bags and moved to Atlanta, a city bustling with opportunities. He began flying and selling airplanes with Aviation Sales Corporation, also known as Corporate Jet Aviation. His hard work and charm paid off quickly. By 1975, just a year later, Tommy had become the President of the company. The title filled him with pride and a sense of accomplishment.

One of his fondest memories from those early days in Atlanta was his first jet sale. "The first jet I sold in Atlanta was a Saber 40 (Sabreliner, Series 40). I loved this jet and thought it was one of the best on the market at the time," Tommy would often recall. The Saber 40, though previously owned, looked brand new and had low flight miles. He sold it to The Allman Brothers Company, No Exit Music, marking the beginning of his exciting journey in the world of high-profile clients. This was even before he started flying Greg Allman and the band.

The doors to Tommy's future were just beginning to open. He fondly remembers, "This is also when I met and became the pilot for Jimmy and Roslyn Carter. Mr. Carter was the Governor of Georgia at the time and was running for President of the United States. I would fly the Carters together or separately, depending on their needs for the day. The jet was a Citation Lear Jet with 8-10 seats. It was a pretty jet with an extremely comfortable ride."

Jimmy Carter served as the Governor of Georgia from 1970 to 1975 before running for President. In 1976, he was elected as the 39th President of the United States. Tommy flew the Carters during the latter part of Carter's governorship and throughout his presidential campaign.

Reflecting on those days, Tommy's emotions run deep, especially as Mr. Carter now faces serious health challenges and Mrs. Carter battles Alzheimer's. "I have a lot of respect for the Carters," Tommy says with heartfelt emotion. "Mrs. Carter was so down to earth and friendly, she never met a stranger. To be honest, I credit her for President Carter getting elected. The press and everyone else loved her too."

Flying the Carters was a serious responsibility, but there were moments of levity too. Tommy recalls one such incident with a smile. "One day, my co-pilot and I were waiting for Mrs. Carter to board. I was flipping through a Playboy magazine on the plane. Suddenly, Mrs. Carter and the press arrived. In a panic, I tossed the magazine over my head, expecting it to land in an overhead compartment. Instead, it landed half in and half out, right as Mrs. Carter stepped onto the plane. The magazine fell at her feet, open to the centerfold. Thinking quickly, I yelled at the reporters, saying I didn't know which one of them threw the magazine, but it better not appear in the news. My bluff worked, and the incident was never mentioned."

Tommy felt embarrassed about the incident because he knew Mrs. Carter was a good Christian lady. However, it didn't stop him from reading Playboy, though he never brought another copy on the plane when flying with Mrs. Carter.

In 1972, George Wallace, the former Governor of Alabama, was also campaigning for the presidency. During his campaign, Wallace was shot by Arthur Bremer, leading to tighter security measures. The Secret Service included Tommy in their organization, which he found both an honor and a responsibility.

Despite the fun of flying important people and selling planes, Tommy's heart was set on something more exciting. "Once I flew a rock group from Atlanta to Orlando," he reminisced. "This was the beginning of my interest in flying rockers. The excitement surrounding the group was a draw for me. It was the first concert I attended where I wasn't performing. I was so fascinated that I decided I wanted to fly rockers someday. Funny thing is, I don't even remember the group's name."

When Tommy returned to Huntsville, he often helped his cousin Dewey Brazelton, a well-known figure in Huntsville with many business interests. Dewey owned the popular nightclub "The Plush Horse," which featured performers like Kenny Rogers, Ray Charles, Tina Turner, Little Richard, and more. "Being around Dewey was always exciting," Tommy recalls. "One time, Tina Turner was performing, and her backup girls were gorgeous. One caught my eye, Audrey. She was stunning, and I had to ask her out. It was a blow to my ego when she turned me down; I was seldom turned down. She was also the first Black girl I ever asked out."

Life was good for Tommy. He was surrounded by exciting people and doing what he loved—flying. But in 1977, he had a close call that made him pause. "I sold a plane, I think it was a Piper Navajo, to a friend in Huntsville, Alabama. I was supposed to take a commercial flight back to Atlanta, but I changed to a later flight at the last minute because I didn't like the weather forecast. That night, the original flight, Flight 242, crashed. My name was still on the manifest, but I had called my mom to tell her about the change. She got a call about the crash but knew I wasn't on the plane. Still, it scared her because it reminded her how dangerous my job was."

In 1977, shortly after flying the Carters, Tommy left Atlanta for a new opportunity with Rockwell International in Maryland. There, he sold jets and flew in air shows. Ron Spangler at Rockwell offered Tommy the chance to fly new planes and work as a test pilot on turboprop and turbo commander airplanes. The move from Atlanta to Maryland was both exciting and daunting for Tommy, who didn't like being far from home. But the prospect of flying new planes was thrilling.

Tommy recalls testing a new Aero Commander. "I found out the hard way that the hydraulics for the landing gear were faulty. The plane had a bad O-ring in the hydraulic line, causing it to lose pressure. My co-pilot, Deborah, was scared and said we had to prepare for a crash landing. I told her no way! I was scared too, but I used all my training to stay calm. I did a hard belly roll of the plane, which forced the landing gear out into position. Once I was sure it was secure, I landed the plane safely. Deborah was relieved and trusted me completely after that."

Tommy was soon asked to fly in an air show in Oklahoma with Bob Hoover, one of his heroes. "Flying with Bob was a dream come true. At first, I was apprehensive, but Bob put me at ease immediately. He was one of the most down-to-earth famous pilots I'd ever met. I looked forward to each event with Bob because he taught me something new each time, and I loved our conversations."

Becoming a test pilot with Bob Hoover was a pinnacle moment for Tommy. Bob Hoover was a legendary figure in aviation, known for his incredible skills and achievements. As Wikipedia describes him, "... an American fighter pilot, test pilot, flight instructor, and record-setting air show aviator... during World War II and was shot down in 1944 off the coast of France... In 2013, Flying magazine ranked him 10th on its list of the 51 Heroes of Aviation."

Tommy's journey was filled with high-flying adventures and memorable experiences. From selling his first jet in Atlanta to flying governors and rock stars, he lived a life many only dream of. Through it all, his passion for flying and his natural charm opened doors and created lasting memories. And though his path was sometimes unpredictable, it was always guided by his love for the sky and the thrill of flight.

Bob Hoover taught Tommy how to fly smoothly, sharing

wisdom and experience that would prove invaluable. Over dinners, they would discuss air shows and Bob would recount tales of his incredible flights. Tommy hung on every word, soaking in the knowledge and advice that Bob generously shared. Those pointers Bob gave him likely saved Tommy's life on more than one occasion. They became close friends during this time, bonded by their shared Southern roots. Bob Hoover hailed from Nashville, Tennessee, and like Tommy, had started from humble beginnings.

Tommy would often recall, "Bob told me about working in a grocery store in Nashville to pay for his flight lessons. He lived an exciting life, was a test pilot, and became one of the best pilots in history. Despite all his achievements, he was one of the most down-to-earth pilots I had ever met." The last time Tommy saw Bob was just before Tommy moved to Houston; Bob passed away in 2016, leaving behind a legacy that deeply influenced Tommy.

While working for Rockwell, Tommy sold over 70 new planes, a remarkable achievement that earned him significant rewards. Each plane sold brought in a hefty commission of about $24,000, along with trophies and recognition from peers in the airplane industry. Despite these accomplishments, Tommy remained humble about his life, often downplaying the excitement and success he experienced.

Tommy never saw his life as particularly special, but to most people, it seemed like an adventurous and thrilling way to live. I still love to listen to his stories, each one a vivid chapter in his fascinating journey. Maybe in time, we can learn more and share those stories with everyone, keeping the spirit of Tommy's adventures alive for future generations.

Tommy's time with Bob Hoover was more than just a professional relationship; it was a mentorship that shaped his flying career. Bob's stories of his own journey, from working in a grocery store to becoming one of history's best pilots, were a testament to what passion and perseverance could achieve. Tommy would often reminisce about the life lessons Bob imparted, lessons that extended beyond the cockpit and into everyday life.

One of Tommy's favorite stories to share was about a piece of advice Bob gave him during a particularly turbulent flight. "Bob told me, 'Tommy, always keep your cool. The plane knows what to do; you just have to guide it.' That bit of wisdom stuck with me and helped me through many rough flights."

Working at Rockwell, Tommy not only honed his skills as a pilot but also proved his prowess in sales. Selling over 70 planes was no small feat, and each sale was a testament to his dedication and hard work. The trophies and commissions were nice, but for Tommy, the real reward was the recognition from others in the industry. He valued the respect and camaraderie he built with fellow pilots and aviation professionals.

Despite his achievements, Tommy's humility shone through. He often said, "I'm just a country boy who got lucky." But those who knew him understood that it was more than luck—it was his passion, skill, and the support of mentors like Bob Hoover that propelled him to such heights.

Reflecting on his journey, Tommy would often say that the best part of his life was the people he met along the way. Whether it was flying governors, rock stars, or everyday businesspeople, each flight added a unique story to his repertoire. And while he might not see his life as extraordinary, those who heard his tales knew otherwise.

As we sit and listen to Tommy's stories, we are transported to a time of adventure and excitement. His memories are not just his own but have become a part of our shared history. And perhaps, in time, we can share more of these stories, passing on the legacy of Tommy's high-flying life to inspire future generations.

5
Tommy's LOVE of Music!

The Cyclones

TOMMY AND HIS COUSIN James Taylor were only seven months apart and inseparable during their childhood. Growing up, they did everything together, their bond strengthened by shared chores and Sunday lunches at their grandma's, who cooked for the entire family. Can you imagine the warmth of those gatherings? The laughter, the stories shared over a table laden with home-cooked meals. They never tired of each other's company, always eager for the next adventure.

Their adventures included a curious twist—dancing lessons. It was our friend John Howard's mother who insisted he take them, and John, not wanting to suffer alone, roped Tommy in too. Picture it: Tommy, John, and John's sister, shuffling through awkward steps at some lady's house in Five Points. I wonder what was it like, to learn to dance in that historic part of Huntsville, where Pratt Avenue, Homes Avenue, and California Street meet? Today, Five Points is a charming historic district, but back then, it was part of the bustling Dallas Mills District, echoing with the hum of textile mills.

Tommy and John's friendship spanned from first grade at Madison Crossroads Elementary through high school at Sparkman High School. They loved baseball, with John playing second base and Tommy as the catcher. Their camaraderie was evident on and off the field, their bond unbroken by the passing years.

Tommy's relationship with music began reluctantly. His mother made him take piano lessons, which he despised, often crying to be allowed outside to play. But in the seventh grade, a spark was lit by Mr. Reeves, one of our teachers. He taught us all to play the kazoo, but for a select few, he offered more: lessons on the guitar and other instruments. Tommy's cousin James mastered the banjo, John Howard played the saxophone, and soon a small band formed, practicing at Mr. Reeves' house.

Can you imagine the melodies that filled those afternoons? The laughter, the off-key notes gradually harmonizing into something beautiful. They named themselves The

Cyclones—a fitting name for a whirlwind of youthful energy. They played at school events and even managed to snag a few paying gigs.

In 1961, The Cyclones performed at the grand opening of Woody Anderson Ford. It was a big deal for a group of kids. Imagine the thrill they felt, earning $25 each—a fortune at that time. They played at homecoming dances and won talent shows, each victory a testament to their growing skill and confidence. Their music even took them to the small screen, performing on the WHNT channel 19 show, Morning Folks, hosted by the iconic Grady Reeves.

Grady Reeves, with his DJ booth atop the Holiday House Restaurant, was a local legend. He once booked an unknown group for a one-night concert, expecting a modest turnout. Who could have guessed that the group included Johnny Cash, Jerry Lee Lewis, Carl Perkins, and Elvis Presley? It's a wonder, isn't it, how these now-legendary names started in small, humble venues, much like The Cyclones.

The Cyclones also played on a Hillbilly Wagon in Decatur, Alabama, promoting Hillbilly Bread by Sunbeam. They roamed the streets, their music a lively backdrop to the bustling town. But, as the name suggests, The Cyclones were a brief, intense storm of talent and enthusiasm. High school brought new challenges and interests, and the band members drifted apart.

Tommy joined the marching band in the 10th grade but left

it by his final years of high school. James transferred to Hazel Green High School, and though he stayed close to Tommy, their paths diverged. Ricky and John focused on football, while Myrna lost interest in the band. Tommy found a new musical partner in Jerry Smith, and together they joined The Mariteens.

Isn't it fascinating how life pulls us in different directions? Tommy's musical journey continued, shaped by the people he met and the experiences he had. Yet, through all the changes, the early days with The Cyclones remained a cherished memory. What became of that childhood band? Did their paths ever cross again in adulthood, their instruments gathering dust in attics, or did the music live on in their hearts?

Reflecting on those days, one can't help but wonder about the bonds we form in our youth. How do they shape the people we become? And what, if anything, remains of those childhood dreams? Tommy's story is a reminder of the fleeting, yet impactful nature of our early years—a nostalgic, heartfelt journey through time.

The Mariteens

In high school, Tommy's musical journey took another vibrant turn. He became part of a band that resonated with the pulse of the times—Jamie Hurt and The Mariteens, formed in Madison County, AL, in late 1965. Jamie, the lead singer, was none other than Roger Murrah. Johnny Allen played the saxophone, and my Tommy showcased his versatility by playing both bass and trumpet. Ray Brand strummed the guitar, Jerry Smith handled the keyboards, and Ellis Waldon kept the rhythm on drums. It was Jim Bickerstaff and his wife Gladys who coined the name Jamie Hurt for Roger and penned the songs "If Love Could Be Measured" and "Big Brass Horn."

Even among this talented ensemble, Tommy stood out. Can you imagine the skill it took to master both bass and trumpet? Each instrument demanded a unique discipline, yet Tommy made it seem effortless.

The group recorded their songs at the legendary FAME Studios in Muscle Shoals, AL, in early 1966. How exciting it must have been for them, laying down tracks in a studio that had seen so many greats! They toured the Southeast in a blue converted horse bus, their music echoing through small towns and big cities alike. Jamie Hurt and the Mariteens reached number one in Mississippi with "If Love Could Be Measured," and even the B-side, "Big Brass Horn," climbed to number thirteen on the charts.

FAME Studios, a beacon of musical history, started in the mid-60s. Many assume FAME stands for famous, but it actually stands for Florence Alabama Music Enterprises. Located in Muscle Shoals, this area in Northern Alabama is affectionately known as "The Shoals." FAME's house band, the Muscle Shoals Rhythm Section—known as the Swampers—played a pivotal role in the careers of numerous superstars. Can you picture the energy in that studio, where legends like Otis Redding and Aretha Franklin recorded?

According to lore, Duane Allman of the Allman Brothers Band once camped out in the FAME Studios parking lot in 1968. During a lunch break, he taught Wilson Pickett "Hey Jude," which was recorded with Duane on lead guitar. The buzz generated by that session led to Duane's record deal, and the rest, as they say, is history. Imagine the excitement of those early days, with future legends crossing paths in such a humble setting.

Jamie Hurt and the Mariteens were riding a wave of success. They were booked for a concert in Corinth, MS, where they were warned not to go out front due to the throngs of screaming girls. But Tommy and his friend Johnny couldn't resist. They had to see the frenzy for themselves. What was it like, I wonder, to step into that sea of adoring fans? Overwhelmed, they were mobbed, losing their jackets in the chaos. Security managed to retrieve the jackets just in time for the show.

Their popularity soared, with fan clubs in Alabama and Mississippi supporting them. They felt like true rock stars, basking in the adulation of their fans. In a hotel in Corinth, they locked the lead guitarist, Ray Brand—nicknamed "Skinny"—out of the room in his boxer shorts. It was a prank that everyone found hilarious, except Skinny. The girls adored Tommy's Beatles-style haircut, making him the band's most popular member.

Everything seemed to be going perfectly for the band. They anticipated continued success and envisioned their songs topping charts nationwide. But life had other plans. The band disbanded in late 1966 when Roger Murrah enlisted in the Army. Maybe you also wonder why did Roger enlist when the band was on the brink of stardom? Many also taught about this sudden turn of events.

Roger felt the looming threat of being drafted and sent to Vietnam. By enlisting, he hoped to have some control over his destiny, choosing his role rather than leaving it to chance. The

Vietnam War, a conflict between North and South Vietnam, cast a long shadow over many young men's futures during that time.

The Vietnam War was a clash of ideologies, with the North supported by communist nations and the United States and its anti-communist allies backing the South. It was a conflict that spanned two decades, from November 1955 to April 1975. When Roger enlisted, he hoped to avoid the front lines. Yet, fate had its own plans, and he found himself in Vietnam, though not in the heat of battle.

Roger's words paint a vivid picture of his time there: "I was in administration, and I received an Army Commendation Medal for designing a 24-hour in-processing center for officers and enlisted men in Nha Trang, one of three headquarters in the country—an old converted French hotel. In front of it was one of the prettiest beaches in Southeast Asia. At night, we could watch our infantrymen mortaring Viet Cong soldiers in the mountains behind us. I was very blessed with safety. I remember that being the very time I started believing in my mother's prayers."

Tommy eventually shed light on the curious origin of the band name Jamie Hurt and the Mariteens. Roger Murrah had known Jim and Gladys Bickerstaff from his early days in the music business. Gladys, a songwriter, wanted someone to give voice to her creations. She penned "If Love Could Be Measured" and "Big Brass Horn," songs that would become part of the band's legacy.

"The Bickerstaffs were the ones who came up with the name Jamie Hurt," Tommy explained. "They thought it was easier to remember than Roger Murrah. Roger introduced me and the rest of the guys to the Bickerstaffs. Gladys wrote the songs, but it was us guys who composed the melodies. We met the Bickerstaffs when we were rehearsing in Jerry Smith's basement."

Reflecting on those days, one can't help but ponder the nature of dreams and how they are shaped by the world around us. What if Roger hadn't enlisted? Would Jamie Hurt and the Mariteens have become household names? Life is full of such what-ifs, and the story of Tommy and his bandmates is a poignant reminder of the delicate balance between ambition and reality. The melody of their youth, filled with promise and passion, remains an enduring part of their legacy, a testament to the fleeting, yet powerful, moments that define our paths.

Yet, indeed time has a way of moving forward, and it leaves traces of the past etched in our hearts. As of this writing, From the Cyclones James, Tommy, John, and Myrna are still with us. James spent 9 years in the Navy and retired from Delphi. John is now a commercial realtor, and Myrna enjoys a peaceful retirement in Fayetteville, TN. Ricky, however, left us too soon, succumbing to brain cancer. His family's grief was compounded by the theft of his ashes from his mother's house. Sadly only Tommy and Roger are left from The Merriteens.

Life's twists and turns often leave us with more questions than answers like how do we even cope with such profound loss? What memories sustain us when those we love are gone? The story of Tommy, his bandmates, and their journey through music and life is a testament to the resilience of the human spirit. It reminds us that even as we navigate the challenges of today, the echoes of the past continue to shape who we are and who we strive to become.

As you reflect on their story, perhaps you'll find yourself pondering your own path. What dreams have we chased? What names and faces have left an indelible mark on our journey? The melody of our youth, filled with hopes and dreams, still resonates, inviting us all to listen and remember.

6
Secrets of the Rock Star Diaries and More

Aces High

Do you ever wonder what drives a person to leave behind a comfortable, familiar life for one of unpredictability and chaos? That was Tommy. With a heart full of excitement and a thirst for challenge, Tommy flew out to California, where he met with Rock Star Managers Doc McGee and Doug Thayer. These were men who managed legends like Motley Crue and Bon Jovi. He wasn't just there to meet them, though—he was there to convince them that he was the man to fly their rock stars across the country.

Tommy, having sold planes to massive corporations and having dealt with presidents and wealthy moguls, could talk to anyone. But this was different. This was rock 'n' roll. Doc McGee and Doug Thayer managed Mötley Crüe, Bon Jovi, and Def Leppard, some of the wildest bands of the era. But the question Doc and Doug had for him was simple: why would he want to fly around self-absorbed rock stars?

Tommy's answer was just as straightforward. He loved the challenge, the excitement. The more unpredictable, the better. Reflecting on this, do you think you would have the courage to chase after such a daunting dream?

Can you imagine the courage it took for him to step into such a different world? Have you ever faced a situation like Tommy, where you had to convince others of your capabilities in an entirely new arena? With a contract in hand, Tommy flew back to Houston, went to the bank, and bought his first plane—not from any of the companies he had worked for, but from a local airport in Houston. It was a Gulfstream G-1, and he named it Aces High Jet Corporate. Rumor had it that the plane had once belonged to Elvis Presley. Tommy couldn't prove it, but it made for a good story that he likes to tell often.

Mötley Crue

I'll never forget the moment Tommy Beal, a man who once piloted high school friends to Kansas City and transported solemn cargo from Alabama to New York, found himself caught up in the whirlwind of rock and roll. His new venture wasn't just another job—it was an adventure, a leap into the unknown with his common-law wife, Deborah, serving as his flight attendant. Can you imagine the excitement and anticipation they must have felt, venturing into a world so different from their past?

Tommy took pride in his role, even down to the details like decorating his plane with the logos of the bands he flew. The first group? Mötley Crue. Their logo featured a scantily clad cowgirl riding a bomb, reminiscent of World War II bomber plane art. Tommy's plane, an eighteen-seat Gulfstream One, wasn't your typical corporate jet. It was outfitted with beds and sofas, wrapped in a unique black leather interior. He named it "Aces High," a nod to his desire to always be in the skies, just like the flying "Aces" of old.

Unlike the corporate flights where passengers were offered only drinks and perhaps some snacks, on Aces High, the experience depended entirely on the group. Imagine boarding a plane to find not just beverages, but also drugs laid out on the meal trays. The offerings ranged from white wine to Jack Daniels, catering to the band's preferences. How do you think Tommy felt, balancing the line between professional pilot and facilitator of such a wild atmosphere?

Taking off was routine, but landing was always a gamble. Tommy often had to ensure the plane was clear of any leftover drugs, as police searches were a constant threat. "Each time we landed we had to be aware that the police might be waiting to search the plane," he recalled. Did he ever feel a pang of anxiety, knowing that one mistake could lead to serious consequences?

Drugs weren't the only challenge Tommy and Deborah faced. At each stop, groupies swarmed the bands, sometimes boarding the plane. The hotel rooms overflowed with girls and drugs. Despite being propositioned by the groupies, Tommy always declined. Was it out of a sense of loyalty to Deborah, his flight attendant and wife? Or perhaps he simply didn't want to indulge in the chaos?

Deborah, with her past experience, likely wasn't shocked by what she saw. Yet, I never pried into whether she and Tommy participated in any of the wilder activities. Given Tommy's respect for me, he probably wouldn't have told me the full truth anyway. So why push him?

In the vibrant 80s and 90s, the band Mötley Crue lived life on the edge, embodying the very essence of rock and roll. Their escapades extended beyond the stage, often leading them to the high-class strip joints in almost every town they visited. They relished in spending hundreds of dollars, seeking out the most exclusive spots to continue their never-ending party. During concerts, they would distribute passes to eager groupies, some of whom had gone to great lengths—sometimes quite literally—to get backstage access. Can you imagine the frenzy and excitement that surrounded their every move?

Tommy, a seasoned pilot, found himself entangled in this whirlwind lifestyle when he became friends with Heather Locklear, who was married to Tommy Lee at the time. Heather remained in touch with Tommy for several years even after he stopped flying the band. Interestingly, Tommy didn't have the opportunity to fly the band during Tommy Lee's marriage to Pamela Anderson. His time in the cockpit coincided with the Girls-Girls-Girls tour and the Doctor Feel Good Tour, both legendary periods in Mötley Crue's history.

Motley Crue Dr. Feel Good Tour

One unforgettable incident occurred in Chicago. While flying Mötley Crue, the jet was struck by lightning, causing a complete electrical failure. The radio rack, situated right behind Tommy's seat, needed immediate attention. With a calm that belied the situation, Tommy stood up, removed the faulty radio, and replaced it with a spare—all while still flying the plane. This resourcefulness wasn't a fluke; it stemmed from Tommy's meticulous nature and his past experiences with radio failures. He always carried a complete rack of replacements, a true testament to his preparedness and test pilot instincts. What would you have done in Tommy's shoes? Could you remain calm and resourceful under such pressure?

Reflecting on his time with Mötley Crue, Tommy couldn't help but remember the tragic death of Stevie Ray Vaughan. "I was in Alpine Valley when Stevie Ray Vaughan was killed in a helicopter crash," he recounted. "In August 1990, I was there to drop off Mötley Crue and pick up Def Leppard. Stevie Ray had just completed a Wisconsin concert. It was a scary and very sad time for all of us. The Alpine Valley was a dangerous place to fly into and out of." The memory of that tragic night lingered, a stark reminder of the unpredictable dangers that lurked in the world of rock and roll.

But the challenges didn't end with navigating perilous flights. After concerts, the band would hastily board the plane, eager to escape any unwanted attention from the police. Tommy Lee's penchant for mooning the audience didn't sit well with city officials, so it fell upon Tommy to ensure the plane was ready for a swift departure. Can you picture the tension and urgency of those moments, knowing that every second counted?

The band members had a peculiar habit known as air-surfing. They would run from the front to the back of the plane, causing it to rock violently. This might sound amusing at first, but for the pilot and crew, it quickly grew tiresome. Tommy had a clever solution: he instructed the flight crew to don their oxygen masks and raised the cabin altitude just enough to put the band to sleep. It was a surefire way to restore peace and order. How would you have handled such rowdy behavior? Would you have come up with a similar ingenious solution?

One particularly tumultuous night, Nikki Sixx became loud and abrasive, directing his ire at one of the girls on board. As his outbursts escalated, someone begged Tommy to intervene. The suggestion was to roll the plane to force Nikki to sit down, but Tommy had a better idea. He lowered the oxygen levels again, letting everyone sleep a bit longer. When they awoke, the previous chaos was forgotten, replaced by a much-needed calm. In such a high-stress environment, Tommy's ability to think on his feet was invaluable. Could you have maintained such composure and found a peaceful resolution in the midst of such turmoil?

Tommy's adventures with Mötley Crue were filled with wild escapades, unexpected challenges, and moments of profound reflection. His experiences paint a vivid picture of a bygone era, one where rock and roll ruled supreme, and every flight was an adventure waiting to unfold.

Tommy, Steven Tyler, and Deborah

The night Mötley Crüe met Aerosmith backstage at one of their concerts was one for the books. It was an evening filled with the typical trappings of rock star parties: an abundance of girls and a haze of drugs, all crammed into a small dressing room. Amidst the revelry, Steven Tyler shared a humorous anecdote with Tommy Lee. The Aerosmith frontman revealed that the inspiration for their hit song "The Dude Looks Like a Lady" came from a time he mistook Vince Neil for a woman, his long blonde hair causing the confusion in a bar. Can you imagine the laughter and camaraderie that must have filled that room? In November of 1987, during the Girls-Girls-Girls tour, they found themselves in Florida. Doc McGhee, their manager, flew down and treated them to a grand Thanksgiving dinner at their hotel, a rare moment of warmth and normalcy amidst their wild lifestyle.

Def Leppard

Flying Mötley Crüe was a rollercoaster—exciting, thrilling, but utterly exhausting. Tommy thrived in the high-octane atmosphere, yet the relentless pace began to take its toll. He didn't fully grasp how much he needed a break until 1987, when fate intervened. Def Leppard's management reached out, offering him a contract to fly the band during their Hysteria tour. It was a welcome change.

When Tommy flew Def Leppard, their name didn't grace the plane. Instead, it bore the word "Hysteria," a fitting moniker for the monumental tour. Def Leppard quickly became one of Tommy's favorite groups. Unlike the chaotic whirlwind of Mötley Crüe, these guys were kind, respectful, and genuinely pleasant to be around. Yes, there were still girls everywhere—as with all the bands Tommy flew—but there was an unmistakable air of respect and camaraderie with Def Leppard. Can you imagine the relief Tommy must have felt, moving from chaos to a more controlled environment?

Tommy did return to fly Mötley Crüe during their Doctor Feel Good tour. The band's behavior hadn't changed much—they were still the same rowdy, hard-partying troublemakers. Yet, despite the madness, Tommy found the experience undeniably fun. But what about his bond with the band? Had the passage of time and the different dynamics changed anything?

When asked which band partied harder, Def Leppard or Mötley Crüe, Tommy's answer was candid. "I partied a lot with Mötley Crüe; we had a lot of good times. I didn't party as much with Def Leppard because they were a calmer group, not as hardcore as Mötley Crüe." After plunging into the deep end of rock and roll with Mötley Crüe, flying Def Leppard felt like a refreshing reset. Tommy immediately took a liking to the guys. They were down-to-earth, easy to talk to, and genuinely got along well with each other. They made Tommy feel like he was part of their team, a sentiment that meant the world to him.

Def Leppard's Hysteria tour kicked off in Glens Falls, NY. Tommy, who hadn't heard the group play before flying them, quickly became a fast fan. The first band member he met was Joe Elliott. As he showed Joe around the plane, they talked about the band's excitement for the Hysteria tour in America. Tommy found inspiration in Rick Allen, the band's drummer.

Rick was on a comeback from a devastating accident that cost him his left arm. On New Year's Eve 1984, a car wreck nearly took his life. Despite this, Rick's courage and determination to return to drumming were nothing short of remarkable.

Tommy often stood backstage, mesmerized by Rick's drumming. Watching Rick play with one hand and his feet was a fascinating experience. Despite the exhaustion, Rick's resilience shone through. Tommy admired Rick's positive attitude, especially given his handicap. Rick's story was a powerful reminder to Tommy, who faced his own personal health issues. How do you cope with the challenges life throws at you? Can you find strength and inspiration in others' resilience?

Tommy, Joe, and Rick spent much of their free time together, exploring cities like Boston, hitting bars, and sightseeing. They blended in easily, not being instantly recognized, which allowed them to enjoy their time without being swarmed by fans. Tommy, with his long hair and love for rock music, fit right in. They would roam towns, enjoying themselves and making memories. How would you enjoy such freedom, even if you were a part of a famous entourage?

Tommy cherished his time with Def Leppard because they made him feel important. At some concerts, he, Joe, and Rick would ride golf carts through the crowd, unnoticed by fans. It was amusing to Tommy that they could navigate through so seamlessly. As the band's popularity grew, sneaking them to the stage became a creative challenge. They even enlisted the help of Robert Plant from Led Zeppelin to drive them unnoticed to the stage, blending in with the roadie equipment.

Def Leppard's concerts were unique in another way—they served meals backstage for everyone, including the roadies. This wasn't common with most bands, but it showed how much Def Leppard appreciated everyone's hard work. Have you ever experienced a small act of kindness that made a significant difference in your day?

Steve Clark, the guitarist, stood out despite his heavy drinking. He got along well with the band and never caused problems on stage or on the plane. Steve was a classically trained guitarist and a talented songwriter. Tragically, his battle with alcohol led to his untimely death in 1991. The band had given Steve a six-month leave to recover, but instead, he spent it drinking heavily. On January 8th, 1991, he was found dead by his girlfriend. It was a heartbreaking end for a talented musician. What could have been done differently to help Steve? Could more support have made a difference?

Tommy often reminisced about Def Leppard's legendary round stage. Beneath it, dozens of beautiful, naked girls tried to catch the band members' attention. Despite the drugs and alcohol surrounding them, Def Leppard remained focused on delivering great performances. Unlike other bands, they partied discreetly. Most nights, they would fall asleep on the plane after the show, exhausted but satisfied.

Even when things went awry, like the night parts of Tommy's

plane were stolen, Tommy knew he had reliable friends. He reached out to Woody Anderson, a close friend with far-reaching influence. Woody helped recover the plane parts, allowing the tour to resume smoothly. How would you handle a crisis in the middle of a tour? Would you have the connections to solve such problems swiftly?

Woody Anderson was more than just the owner of a large Ford dealership in Huntsville, Alabama. He had a history of significant influence, as evidenced by his involvement in a 1964 plan to attract Black engineers to Huntsville for NASA contracts. Having someone like Woody in his corner was invaluable for Tommy, proving that in the chaotic world of rock and roll, reliable friends were worth their weight in gold.

How do you find balance in your life? What memories stand out as reminders of the importance of kindness and respect? For Tommy, his time with Def Leppard was a mix of excitement, camaraderie, and heartfelt moments. The band's respect and kindness left a lasting impression on him, offering a stark contrast to the wild ride with Mötley Crüe. Through the highs and lows, Tommy found a balance, appreciating the quieter moments amidst the chaos.

Gregg Allman and Cher

Cher

Meeting Gregg Allman and Cher was one of the most unforgettable moments in Tommy's career. Both were larger-than-life figures, yet together, they formed one of the most tortured couples he ever flew. The memory of meeting Cher, in particular, stands out vividly in his mind.

In August 1989, Tommy had the privilege of flying Cher and her then-boyfriend, a dancer named Tony Burgess, for the first leg of her Heart of Stone Tour. It wasn't the first time he had flown Cher, though. Years earlier, when he was based in Atlanta, he had flown her during her tumultuous marriage to Gregg Allman. He doubted Cher remembered him from those days, given the immense stress she endured because of Gregg.

Tommy was working for Corporate Jet Service in Atlanta when he received the exciting news that Gregg Allman and Cher needed a pilot for Gregg's tour. As a fan of Gregg's music and someone who had already sold the Allman Brothers a plane, Tommy was thrilled. He had come to know the Allman Brothers fairly well, but the internal strife within the band, largely due to Gregg allegedly informing the police about their drug activities, had caused them to disband for several years.

Gregg's testimony had led to immunity from prosecution but also required him to be placed in protective custody. This betrayal created a deep rift between him and the rest of the band. Marrying Cher only worsened the situation, as her presence clashed with the band's drug and alcohol-fueled lifestyle. Can you imagine the tension and heartbreak that must have permeated those relationships? How would you handle the betrayal of a close friend, especially in such a high-stakes environment?

Tommy's only flight with Gregg and Cher was filled with drama. Gregg, scheduled for a concert in Atlanta, had disappeared to the Bahamas. Tommy was tasked with flying Cher down to retrieve him. When Cher boarded the plane, Tommy was struck by her beauty and grace. She was courteous and talkative, making the initial part of the journey quite pleasant.

Finding Gregg in the Bahamas was a challenge, especially in the pre-cell phone era. Eventually, they located him, drunk in a bar. Coaxing him onto the plane took some effort, but they finally managed to get airborne. The flight back was tense, with Cher and Gregg arguing the entire way. Yet, once they landed, the atmosphere shifted to a more subdued and pleasant tone.

Backstage at the concert, Tommy spent the evening with Cher, a memory he cherishes deeply. It was one of the best times he ever had with a woman when they were both sober and fully present. They talked about everything and nothing, and Tommy was struck by how down-to-earth and easy to talk to she was, unlike many other entertainers he had met. Despite the grandeur of her stage presence, Cher's small stature surprised him. Though some claimed she was 5'9", Tommy estimated she was closer to 5'5". She certainly looked taller under the stage lights.

Shortly after that memorable evening, Tommy learned that Cher was expecting a baby with Gregg. However, the tour was abruptly canceled due to Gregg's erratic behavior, and Tommy didn't get another chance to fly them. Cher later reflected on her time with Gregg, describing him as the love of her life—a Southern gentleman who respected and adored her. Despite her efforts to help him overcome his addictions, the toll on their marriage proved too great.

I always think about how the pressures of fame and personal struggles can affect one's family dynamics? Cher and Gregg's love story was a whirlwind. They married only a couple of months after her divorce from Sonny Bono. At the time, Cher had a daughter from her marriage to Sonny, named Chastity Bono. In 2009, Chastity came out as a trans man and transitioned to Chaz Bono. In 1976, Cher and Gregg welcomed their son, Elijah Blue Allman, who inherited his parents' musical talent and even played guitar on stage with Cher a few times.

Tommy's experiences with Gregg and Cher left an indelible mark on him. Their story was one of passion, turmoil, and fleeting moments of peace—a stark reminder of the complex, often painful realities behind the glamorous façade of celebrity life.

Bon Jovi European Tour

Bon Jovi

In 1989, Tommy received news that filled him with excitement and anticipation. He was to fly Bon Jovi on their European tour. Overwhelmed with joy, Tommy poured his energy into revamping his plane, making all the changes he believed the band would appreciate. Meeting Jon Bon Jovi, a man whose voice and energy had always captivated him, was a thrilling prospect. He meticulously stocked the plane with everything he had been told Bon Jovi wanted, eager to make a stellar impression.

However, Tommy's excitement quickly faded as he realized Bon Jovi viewed him merely as hired help. This was a stark contrast to his experience with Def Leppard, who had treated him like part of their family. The clash of egos between Tommy and Jon Bon Jovi became apparent almost immediately. Nothing Tommy did seemed to please Jon, and this friction extended to the rest of the crew, causing mounting frustration.

Adding to Tommy's stress was the fact that this was his first international trip. He had built up great expectations, only to be let down by Jon Bon Jovi's constant dissatisfaction. One incident, in particular, stood out. Due to rough weather, Tommy instructed the crew to serve drinks in plastic glasses during a meal. Jon Bon Jovi, enraged by this, threw his drink into the server's face, shouting, "I don't drink out of plastic." The server was Tommy's brother-in-law, Stan. This act of disrespect pushed Tommy to the edge, casting a perpetual cloud over his interactions with Jon.

The tension reached new heights while in England. Jon Bon Jovi, accustomed to drinking cranberry juice regularly, demanded it, but it was unavailable everywhere. Determined to meet his demand, Tommy found a place willing to grind the berries into juice for a steep price of $2,500—a significant sum in 1989. Jon didn't care about the cost, and Tommy, driven by a desire to appease him, paid the price.

Have you ever faced a situation where your pride clashed with practicality? For Tommy, he had placed Jon Bon Jovi on a pedestal, investing heavily in preparing the plane to meet his high standards, only to be met with complaints and arguments. The breaking point came in England when Tommy, fed up with the constant bickering, decided to have Jim Worthington, another pilot, fly over to complete the tour. Tommy's pride wouldn't let him concede at the time, but in hindsight, he realized that perhaps he should have gone along with whatever

Jon wanted.

Despite the rocky tour, there were silver linings. Tommy and some of the crew spent Christmas in London, courtesy of Bon Jovi. They stayed in one of the nicest hotels Tommy had ever seen, indulged in shopping, clubbing, and sightseeing. This downtime offered Tommy a chance to reflect on the tumultuous flights. He began to see that Bon Jovi, experiencing his own pressures from the fast rise in popularity and the challenges of his first international tour, was as tense as Tommy. Both had wanted everything to be perfect, leading to their clash.

When the tour ended, Tommy and his crew flew back home on one of Tommy's planes, leaving the Bon Jovi tour as a mere memory. Reflecting on the experience, Tommy hoped that if he and Jon Bon Jovi met today, they could become friends, both having aged and gained more patience.

In the end, Tommy's experience with Bon Jovi was a lesson in humility and patience, underscoring the importance of understanding and adapting to others' expectations. It was a chapter filled with high tension and valuable insights, a testament to the complexities of navigating egos in the high-stakes world of rock and roll.

Metallica was the last rock group Tommy flew. He said he only flew them for a few concerts because his mind wasn't on flying right then and he always believed that you had to be in a good place mentally to take to the skies. He had some of his other pilots take over and finish the tour. He said they had so much energy and comradery with each other that it was impossible not to like being around them, but again his mind was on things going on in his personal life and to be very honest, the drugs had become a part of his everyday life. He had to find a way to beat that addiction. He says he never flew before or after the drugs, but that was part of his reason for quitting the group, he wanted the drugs more than anything else right then.

METALLICA

James Brown

James Brown, the legendary "Godfather of Soul" and the "Hardest Working Man in Show Business," was one of the most fascinating men Tommy ever had the privilege of flying. While working for Corporate Jet Aviation in Atlanta, Tommy received the thrilling news that James Brown needed a pilot and co-pilot for an unscheduled concert in Gadsden, Alabama. The opportunity to fly Mr. Brown's plane, a De Havilland Jet, was a chance Tommy couldn't pass up.

"Unlike flying rockers, James Brown was exciting and electrifying to be around," Tommy recalled. "There were beautiful girls everywhere, and I would just stand in amazement at the noise and thrill of everything that was happening. Flying James Brown was some of the most fun I ever had. There was never a dull moment around James Brown. He always made sure everyone was taken care of in a lavish way."

Tommy was eager to take the flight for two reasons: he had never flown a De Havilland before, and he was captivated by the aura surrounding Mr. Brown. James Brown was the first Black entertainer to own an airplane. His first plane was a smaller Lear Jet, but the De Havilland was larger and more impressive. Although the flight from Atlanta to Gadsden was short, Tommy cherished the brief time he spent with Mr. Brown. "It was great to meet him in person; he was very nice to me and our crew," Tommy said. "His backup singers were also on board, and as you can imagine, they were beautiful."

Have you ever wondered about the behind-the-scenes moments that make up the lives of such iconic figures? One thing that stood out during these flights was Mr. Brown's insistence on paying cash for everything, including the fuel. Tommy observed a lot of money changing hands among the people on board. Upon landing in Gadsden, fans were eagerly waiting to catch a glimpse of Mr. Brown and his band. There were many pretty girls around, likely groupies, but Tommy didn't leave the airport to see what unfolded after the band left.

The return flight to Atlanta was memorable in its own way. They had Kentucky Fried Chicken on board, which Tommy loved, although it left a strong smell in the plane. Despite the brief interaction, Tommy's experience with James Brown was overwhelmingly positive. It contrasted sharply with the media portrayal of Mr. Brown at the time. In 1998, James Brown made headlines for leading the police on a two-state car chase in Georgia. In the decade prior, he had been arrested multiple times for various offenses, including drug possession, domestic abuse, and discharging a firearm in an insurance company office. Yet, Tommy never saw Mr. Brown do anything negative. There was no drinking, smoking, or drugs allowed on the plane.

Reflecting on this period, Tommy couldn't help but feel a sense of admiration for James Brown. The entertainer's ability to captivate and care for those around him, despite the controversies that surrounded his life, was a testament to his complex character.

Tommy's flights with James Brown remain etched in his memory as a unique chapter in his aviation career. The experience was a blend of awe, excitement, and respect, offering a glimpse into the life of a man who was as legendary for his music as he was for his larger-than-life personality. It was a reminder that even those who seem untouchable on stage are human, with all the complexities and contradictions that come with it.

Eric Burton of The Animals

Recalling his time with Eric Burdon of The Animals is an emotional journey for Tommy. Their connection transcended the usual pilot-musician dynamic; it felt more like a bond between two best friends. Despite Eric's fame as a singer-songwriter, when they were together, he was just a regular person. Tommy flew Eric several times, but never the other members of the band. Their friendship was unique and special.

How often do we find such unwavering trust in our friendships? Eric, a few years older than Tommy, had a youthful spirit that made him fun to be around. They clicked instantly, sharing an energy that felt like the promise of an endless friendship. Both had a passion for riding motorcycles, often embarking on rides when they weren't flying or touring. One unforgettable adventure in Arizona saw them riding into the hills, where Eric acquired some peyote. They got pretty messed up, and Tommy still doesn't remember how they got the peyote or made it back to the hotel. This wild escapade was a testament to Eric's trust in Tommy—a trust that came from being a famous star and believing that his friend would always take care of him without betrayal.

How does fame change a person, if at all? Is it possible to remain grounded and approachable like Eric did? Tommy wasn't wealthy, and since the rest of The Animals traveled by bus between gigs, he only charged Eric for the plane's fuel. He flew Eric to Colorado and around Arizona for various club concerts, cherishing those memories. "We sat around watching him perform, and believe me, the guy could entertain a crowd. Yes, there were always a lot of women, but Eric wasn't married during the '80s, and he was so down-to-earth and easy to talk to that everyone around him was captivated—especially the women," Tommy reminisced.

Another hallmark of their friendship was their shared reminiscing about growing up in the sixties and seventies—a time marked by chaos and wild adventures. They often marveled at how they had survived those tumultuous years. Eric confided in Tommy about his feelings toward his hit song, "The House of The Rising Sun." Despite its success, Eric hated singing it but knew it was his moneymaker and had to keep performing it. This revelation added a poignant layer to the song's opening lyrics: "There is a house in New Orleans, They call the Rising Sun, And it's been the ruin of many a poor boy, And God I know I'm one."

The bond between Tommy and Eric was more than just a series of shared experiences; it was a deep and genuine friendship that left a lasting impact on Tommy's life. They shared secrets, wild adventures, and quiet moments of reflection—experiences that built a friendship that was as real offstage as it was in the spotlight. Reflecting on such friendships, we are reminded of the importance of trust, understanding, and shared histories.

Nikko McBain of Iron Maiden

When Tommy talks about how he met Nikko McBrain, the drummer of Iron Maiden, his eyes light up with a vibrant glow. Nikko was the spark that ignited Tommy's journey into the world of rock and roll. Their paths crossed at Jeff Hammer's store, Texas Tapes and Records, a haven for rock bands to sign records and meet fans. It was there that Jeff introduced Tommy to Nikko, and with both being party enthusiasts, they hit it off immediately, forming a fast and lasting friendship.

"It was Nikko who suggested I fly rockers," Tommy recalls fondly. "He was the one who told me who to contact in LA. We often partied at Jeff Hammer's house, and later, when Nikko and his wife Rebecca were in town, they would stay at my house in Houston. Nikko loved to fly, and we would go flying for a whole day." Can you imagine the thrill of having a rock legend as a close friend and flying companion?

Seeing the spark in Tommy's eyes as he recounts his adventures with Nikko is heartwarming. They flew to many different places, meeting famous musicians like Joan Jett, Eric Clapton, Robert Plant, and Lita Ford. The entire Iron Maiden group were genuinely nice guys who loved their craft. At an Iron Maiden concert in London, a beach ball thrown from the crowd hit Tommy's hand, almost breaking his thumb. The medical team put frozen peas on his hand. Nikko had warned him about the flying beach balls, but Tommy hadn't paid attention.

One particularly funny story Tommy shares is about a hotel in LA. "Nikko, Jeff Hammer, and I ran through the halls putting funny stickers on doors. Nikko rented out a theme attraction, Wally World, so we could ride all the rides without fans bothering us." Their antics highlight the playful side of rock stardom, a world where even legendary musicians sought moments of normalcy and fun.

Though Tommy wasn't Iron Maiden's official pilot, he often flew with Nikko as his copilot. Sometimes, Nikko would take the controls, and Tommy would sit back as the copilot. One memorable flight back to Houston from LA with Nikko, Jeff, and a few others onboard, Tommy forgot to reset the altimeter after refueling in Denver. The altimeter readings were off, which could have been disastrous. "It took me a couple of minutes to realize it, and everyone thought it was funny at the time. However, the thought that we could have been the headlines for another rock-n-roll plane crash did not escape me."

After Tommy left Houston, he and Nikko lost touch but reconnected a few years ago. Tommy still holds Nikko in high regard as a great friend and person. In 2019, Tommy planned to attend a concert in Nashville to meet up with Nikko, but a mini-stroke just days before the event thwarted his plans. Despite this setback, the hope remains that they will reconnect in person someday.

What are the memories you hold dear with your closest friends, and how have they shaped your journey? Tommy's friendship with Nikko McBrain was more than just a professional connection; it was a deep, personal bond that significantly impacted his life. Their shared adventures and mutual respect illustrate the profound effect that true friends can have, leaving lasting impressions and cherished memories.

Nine-Eleven

The images from September 11, 2001—known universally as Nine-Eleven—are etched into the minds of not only Americans but people all over the world. The sight of the Twin Towers in New York City engulfed in flames is an image that has become a permanent fixture in our collective consciousness. Watching civilians flee from the destruction while every Fire Department, Police Department, and first responders rushed toward the chaos was a poignant testament to the spirit of America that day.

It was a Tuesday, September 11, 2001, at 8:46 a.m. Eastern Time, when the world changed forever. American Airlines Flight 11 crashed into the North Tower of the World

Trade Center. The plane, en route from Boston's Logan International Airport to Los Angeles, carried ninety-two souls. Initially, there was confusion; was it an accident? But as news spread, the horrifying reality set in. At 9:03 a.m., United Airlines Flight 175 struck the South Tower with sixty-five souls on board.

Four commercial aircraft were hijacked that day. At 9:37 a.m., American Airlines Flight 77 crashed into the western façade of the Pentagon, carrying fifty-nine souls. The final blow came at 10:07 a.m. when United Airlines Flight 93 went down in a field in Somerset County, Pennsylvania. Forty courageous passengers and crew fought back against the hijackers, preventing the plane from reaching its intended target. The decision to reclaim their flight or die trying immortalized their bravery.

In total, nearly 3,000 lives were lost in the initial crashes and the subsequent collapse of the Twin Towers. At 9:42 a.m., the FAA grounded all flights over or bound for the continental United States—a historic first. Over the next two and a half hours, 3,300 commercial flights and 1,200 private planes were guided to the nearest airports in Canada and the United States. Amid this unprecedented shutdown, Tommy was called upon to help .

Since 1999, Tommy had been flying med-flights, a role he found both fulfilling and challenging. A call from Roy Horridge, a long-time pilot friend from Houston, had introduced him to this line of work. "Flying medical patients sounded interesting," Tommy recalled, "since I had once flown dead bodies; flying live ones seemed better." While he enjoyed the opportunity to save lives, the job was more stressful than he anticipated.

One of his most memorable flights involved retrieving a critically injured teenage girl from Mexico after an ATV accident. "She was in such bad shape that I wasn't sure she'd make it back alive. I got her to Phoenix, but I never heard whether she made it or not. I've thought about her many times over the years and hoped she was able to live a full life." Most medical flights carried critically ill patients with doctors and nurses working tirelessly to keep them alive throughout the journey.

When the attacks occurred, Tommy, like the rest of the world, learned of them through news reports. As a pilot, he could vividly imagine the terror and chaos the crews of the hijacked planes must have experienced. The thought was deeply unsettling, shaking him to his core. Despite his own turmoil, he was called upon to perform his duty, a responsibility he did not take lightly.

Tommy recalls his involvement with a heavy heart. "The whole country was in shock, and there was a sense of helplessness that permeated everything. But we had to keep moving forward. I was assigned to assist in the aftermath, flying critical supplies and personnel to where they were needed most. The skies were eerily quiet except for our planes, which were filled with a somber urgency."

"On September 11, 2001, I received a call that afternoon to fly to Chicago, Illinois, to pick up a patient in critical condition and fly him back to Phoenix. My emotions were all over the place, realizing we were one of a handful of planes allowed to fly that day. The skies were eerily empty and somber, filled with an overwhelming sadness. At the same time, it was exciting and scary because everyone in the world was watching the very few planes in the air.

Only Med-Flight or emergency medical transport planes were allowed to fly; all others were grounded until September 13. The world had come to a standstill because of a handful of terrible people who tried to destroy our freedom. Knowing F-16s were closely monitoring our flight was both a concern and a comfort, making me feel safer. I flew several other medical flights over the next few weeks, always aware of the terror that could strike at any moment."

The days following Nine-Eleven were a blur of nonstop flights and logistical coordination. Tommy and his fellow pilots transported medical teams, equipment, and relief supplies to New York and other affected areas. Each flight carried not just the weight of its cargo but also the collective grief and determination of a nation in mourning.

Tommy felt grateful to help during this challenging time in the nation's history. None of his med-flight patients were a direct result of the Nine-Eleven attacks, and he considered himself blessed that none of his family or friends were victims in The Towers. However, Tommy experienced a frightening incident during one of these med-flights, which he now refers to as his "hard landing story."

"I had just transported a critical patient to Chicago from Phoenix. The flight medical team and I were on our way back to Phoenix when I lost ALL power to the Lear Jet. It was a nighttime flight, and we were flying through thick clouds. There were no two ways about it—we were going down, and I was doing everything I knew to get the power back on.

Crashing wasn't on my mind. I was fighting to save my passengers and land the plane safely. I said a prayer, asking God to give me the knowledge to restore power and save the medical team on board. Truly, I wasn't thinking about myself at that point.

God heard my prayer, and when we were down to about three or four thousand feet, the power suddenly came back on. Our landing was a bit rough, but we landed safely in Missouri. We stayed on the ground overnight and ensured the electrical system received a thorough inspection.

It's hard to admit that I was scared, but everything happened so fast. I was trying everything I knew to restore power. I didn't even have time to inform the doctors and nurses on board about what was happening. Given how quickly we were descending, I'm sure they knew something was wrong. I wasn't about to fly out of Missouri without ensuring everything was fixed. It was a complete electrical failure—nothing was working! After repairs the next day, we were flying again. The medical team were troopers, probably because they deal with life and death every day."

How do we find the courage to face our deepest fears? Tommy's recollections of Nine-Eleven and the weeks that followed highlight the bravery and dedication of those who rose to the occasion in the face of unprecedented tragedy. His own experience during the hard landing is a testament to his resilience and the faith that carried him through. In moments of crisis, we often discover strengths we didn't know we had and find solace in the belief he was not alone.

His experience of Nine-Eleven was a defining moment in his life and career. It was a time of profound sorrow, immense responsibility, and unyielding resolve. The memories of that day and the days that followed are forever etched in his mind, serving as a reminder of the resilience and courage displayed by so many. As he reflects on his role during that dark time, Tommy's story is a testament to the unbreakable spirit of those who rose to the occasion when the world needed them most.

7
Fate Finally Found Its Way To Us

SOMETIMES, LIFE HAS A funny way of changing your path. What seems like a good thing can turn out bad, and sometimes something bad turns out good. One way to say it is, "What the devil meant for bad, God meant for good."

Looking back, I see how true that saying is. Most people would think a heart attack is something bad, and I would agree. But this was one of those times when God used a bad situation to turn it into something good, something that would change my life and my path forever. It was a chilly March morning in 2003 when I ended up having a minor heart attack. It sounds strange to say "minor" and "heart attack" in the same sentence, doesn't it? The simple truth is, I had a heart attack. Thankfully, it didn't kill me, but it shook me to my core. I continued to have some health issues, so my doctor sent me to Huntsville Hospital for a check-up and tests to make sure I was okay.

As I walked through the familiar halls of Huntsville Hospital, a wave of nostalgia washed over me. I had spent many hours here, both as a visitor and a patient. The sterile scent of antiseptic mixed with the faint aroma of coffee from the cafeteria brought back a flood of memories. I was lost in my thoughts, contemplating what the test results might reveal, when I felt a strange awareness, like someone was trying to get my attention. Someone was calling my name, no, they were calling me by my maiden name. "Barbara Ann... Barbara Ann Jacks, is that you?"

I turned around, my heart pounding, to see who it was. And there she stood, a figure from my past, looking just as I remembered. "Mrs. Giles?" I asked slowly, my voice trembling, "Dot, is that you?" She smiled, one of those nearly crying smiles, and nodded her head up and down while opening her arms for a big, welcoming hug.

Hugging me with the warmth of a mother was Mrs. Dorothy Giles, or Dot, as everyone called her. She was Tommy Beal's mother, a woman whose kindness and strength had left a lasting impression on everyone who knew her. Dot had married Jimmy Giles when Tommy was eleven years old. Mr. Giles was a coroner and worked at Laughlin Funeral Home. I remember Jimmy often telling us with a chuckle that one of the benefits of being a coroner was that when a prominent businessman in Huntsville died, he got his shoes. He always said they were the best shoes he ever had.

Later, Jimmy worked at Woody Anderson Ford as a service manager. The transition from working at a funeral home to managing a service department at the largest dealership around came with its own set of challenges and rewards. Woody Anderson was a powerful figure in Huntsville, known for his philanthropy and behind-the-scenes influence in politics. It was said that when Black engineers came to Huntsville to work as part of the space program, they struggled to find hotel rooms due to segregation. Woody Anderson, along with other community leaders and Senator John Sparkman, opened The Kings Inn Hotel, allowing Black people to stay there. This act of quiet defiance and support wasn't widely known until many years later, when Bob Ward, a former editor of the Huntsville Times, wrote about it.

Woody Anderson became a close friend to the Giles family. I remember Dot telling me how Woody provided her with a car so she wouldn't have to use her own while delivering mail. If the weather was bad, he would let Jimmy off so he could help drive her route. Dot didn't date anyone for years after Tommy's father passed away. Her first serious relationship after that was with Chester McCutcheon. They had planned to get married, but Dot's mother was adamant that she would not marry him. Dot believed it was because Chester was divorced and had a child. She often said that Chester was the love of her life, and it broke her heart when their relationship ended.

Dot eventually met Jimmy Giles through mutual friends. Jimmy was a likable guy with a great sense of humor and seemed to know everybody in town. They decided to get married when Tommy was eleven. I still remember the day of their wedding; Tommy came running to our house, beaming with excitement, telling me he had a new dad. Jimmy was always there for Tommy, supporting him in all his endeavors, especially his passion for flying.

Later, Jimmy's position at Woody Anderson Ford brought a certain amount of prestige and a better income. Woody Anderson was a significant figure in Huntsville, not just for his business acumen but also for his contributions to the community and his political influence. He played a crucial role in supporting the Black engineers who came to Huntsville during the space race, a story that only came to light many years later. Woody helped Tommy several times with his music and when his airplane needed repairs, proving to be a steadfast friend to the Giles family.

Dot herself was an incredible woman. She became a pilot in her late fifties, flying out of the airport on Redstone Arsenal. Everyone said she was an excellent pilot, although Tommy never got the chance to fly with her, something they both regretted. Jimmy later developed Alzheimer's and passed away in 2004. Dot's memory began to fade, and she moved in with us a few months before she died in 2021. Tommy's brother Donny had passed away in 2019 from unknown causes, adding another layer of sorrow to Dot's later years.

As I stood there in the hospital hallway, hugging Dot and reminiscing about the past, I realized how much these people had shaped my life. My heart attack had brought me back to this place, to this moment, reconnecting me with a cherished friend from my past. What seemed like a bad thing had turned into a blessing, reminding me of the strength and resilience of the human spirit, and the enduring bonds of friendship and family.

Life indeed has a funny way of changing your path. What the devil meant for bad, God truly meant for good.

Standing there in the hospital, Dot looked tired and much older than I would have expected, but it was her, and oh, what a wonderful sight to behold. Her hair, now a soft gray, framed her face in a way that spoke of years gone by and countless memories shared. I felt a sudden need to be close to her, to reconnect with someone who had been such an integral part of my childhood. She hugged me with a familiar warmth, the kind of hug that wraps around your heart and makes you feel safe.

Dot and I had spent so much time together when I was growing up. She would bake the most delightful tea cakes, knowing they were my favorite. The aroma of those freshly baked treats would waft through her kitchen, drawing me in. She'd call me over as soon as they were ready, and we'd sit and chat about everything and nothing. Our conversations would meander through the events of the day, what I was up to, and what Tommy was doing. She was always there, a steadfast presence, ready to listen and offer her wisdom.

As we stood talking in the hospital hallway, catching up on each other's lives, it felt like stepping back in time. The years melted away, and we were just two old friends, sharing stories and memories. But soon, our conversation turned to why Dot was at the hospital. With a heavy heart, she told me that Tommy had suffered a massive stroke and was struggling to recover.

The worry etched on her face was unmistakable. I had heard that Tommy had gotten married, and I shared with her that I didn't want to intrude on his family. That's when she told me he was alone, having been divorced for several years. A part of me was afraid he wouldn't remember me, which would have just crushed me. I had loved him from afar all my life.

Dot's encouragement was gentle but firm. She really wanted me to see him. I hesitated, but deep down, I knew I had to go. Walking into his room that day, a whirlwind of emotions swirled inside me—fear, doubt, insecurity. What would he say? What would I say? Would he even remember me? Would I still be important to him as he was to me?

Tommy and I hadn't seen each other in over forty years; the last time was in a nightclub in Huntsville. I was with my husband Don, his sister, and her husband. We had been to a wedding for a friend and decided to stop in for a drink. I spotted Tommy as I went to the bathroom. We chatted for a couple of minutes, keeping it short because we both knew Don's temper. Don was a very jealous man, and Tommy didn't want me to get in trouble.

Growing up, Tommy and I were more than just friends. We shared a bond that went deeper than most. After his stroke, we began talking on the phone weekly. After my divorce, we even talked about getting together, but it took a couple of years to make that decision. I had to find myself before I could commit to him as his wife. I had loved him for as long as I could remember. He was my best friend for so many years, and my feelings for him had never wavered. I knew I wanted him in my life.

As I entered his room, the first thing that caught my attention was the monitors beeping rhythmically. But when Tommy saw me, his face lit up with a smile, and his blue eyes sparkled, just as they had when we were young.

Walking into Tommy's hospital room was like stepping back in time. He couldn't talk at the time, but his beautiful blue eyes and smile told me he remembered me. Trying to convey the flood of emotions I felt at that moment is impossible, but it felt like coming home. Seeing his blue eyes took me back to our early days and how he'd look at me when we were together. My heart and mind returned to when we were each other's best friends.

I later learned that on the day Tommy had his stroke, he had flown back from Key West and had only been home a couple of hours when he told his roommate that he had the worst pain in his head and neck he'd ever felt. At the time, Tommy shared a house in Double Springs, Alabama, about seventy-five miles southeast of Huntsville, with his friend Rick Martin. Tommy fell on his bedroom floor upstairs, making a loud bang. Rick heard it and ran upstairs. Tommy was unable to move or speak, but his eyes were open. Rick called 911; they took Tommy to Cullman Hospital, and they decided to transport him by ambulance to Huntsville Hospital. It was an hour's drive, and they couldn't fly him because they feared the aneurysm would start bleeding again. It was touch and go for over a month.

Tommy was on a respirator, unable to move anything but one finger. After a month, he started coming around, but they kept him on the respirator until one day he pulled it out himself. He said he wanted to talk.

His mom said they called a code, and she saw nurses running toward his room. She was afraid something terrible had happened to Tommy. After the excitement, they let Dot go in, and there he was grinning from ear to ear, still unable to talk but coming back.

After I saw him that day in the hospital, his mom would call and keep me posted on his progress. When he could talk again, he and I would talk on the phone a couple of times a week. I was still married then, but I wasn't going to let Don's jealousy keep me from being there for my best friend. Don was extremely jealous, and it didn't take much to set him off. This happened my entire marriage. But my friend needed me at the darkest time in his life. Tommy went through extensive physical, occupational, and speech therapy; he couldn't talk or walk for a while. He regained his speech and limited walking abilities after several intensive months. Although we spoke on the phone because of work, I spent my free time with my mom and granddad. I didn't see him again in person until 2011, eight years later.

Seeing Tommy in the hospital allowed me to focus more on my life. Although I didn't see him, I talked to his mom, and she told me when he could speak again. He fought hard to regain his ability to walk and talk; even using his arms was limited when he left the hospital. His mom said that after seeing me in the hospital, he became more determined to regain his strength. Tommy said he was at his lowest when he had the stroke, and seeing me made him want to fight to get better. Talking to his mom helped me know how he was doing.

As Tommy and I talked on the phone, I could tell he was getting better, but it was a struggle for him, and there were days when he sounded like he wanted to give up. I couldn't let him do that. We would talk to each other like when we were kids. He went through a depression because he was fighting to get better, and it was a slow process. But like Tina Turner, Tommy didn't do anything slow and easy.

I'd found my best friend after 40 years, and I didn't want to lose him again. He was in rehab for several months and then allowed to go home to his mom's house, where he continued to fight to get better. The days turned into weeks, and the weeks into months. Each day was a struggle for Tommy, but his spirit remained unbroken. He was determined to reclaim his life, one painstaking step at a time. It occurred to me more than once that we waited 40 years apart, and it was possible that we missed any chance to be happy together. Those thoughts haunted me during quiet moments, the weight of lost time pressing heavily on my heart. It was eight long years after that day I saw him in the hospital that I finally saw him in person again. The best I could do during those years was talk to him and his mother on the phone, cherishing each conversation as a lifeline to the past and a promise for the future.

My family has always been a guiding star in the course of my love life. My mom and dad were high school sweethearts, deeply committed to each other. We grew up witnessing the quiet, steadfast love they shared. Their love was a tapestry woven with threads of patience, understanding, and unwavering support. None of us ever saw or heard them arguing, even though Mom said they had their moments. They had an unspoken agreement to keep their disputes private, shielding us from any turbulence. I longed for a relationship like theirs but didn't find it until Tommy and I got back together.

It was my brother Steve who gave me the courage to seek happiness. Steve was my rock, always ready with advice and a shoulder to lean on. He stressed that life wasn't a certainty and that we shouldn't waste time being unhappy. When I confided in him about my conversations with Tommy, he was unwavering in his support. He told me I needed to decide if I would stay in a miserable marriage or finally gather the courage to divorce Don. Losing Steve to cancer in 2011 was a low point in my life, a chasm of grief that seemed impossible to cross. It was just him, Mom, and me here in Huntsville for a long time. My brothers Donald, Clark, and Larry lived out of town. Steve died in June, and that same month, I told Don that I wanted a divorce. Don's reaction was as volatile as I feared. He was so angry that he called Tommy, demanding that he leave me alone. I think he thought that if Tommy were out of the picture, I would stay with him. But Tommy, ever the gentleman, told Don that we were friends and that he'd always be there for me. Although Tommy was distraught with the way Don treated me, he never pressured me to divorce him.

My daughters did not meet Tommy until after my divorce from Don. They had grown up in a household marked by tension, and I wanted their first meeting with Tommy to be free of the shadows of the past. Tommy began getting his strength back and was motivated to try to fly again. Still, as one thing got better, another medical issue would arise. When he developed macular degeneration, he knew his flying days were over. It was a heartbreaking realization for him, and I could see the pain in his eyes as he talked about it. At that point, I knew he needed me more than ever. The dreams he once soared within the skies now needed to find new wings on the ground.

Over time, I learned more about the life Tommy lived while we were apart, including his first marriage. In Atlanta, Tommy discovered a penchant for strip clubs, an escape from the loneliness that often accompanied his travels. He frequented them regularly, finding solace in the vibrant, albeit transient, company. Once he moved to Maryland from Atlanta, he inquired about local strip clubs, and one of his coworkers suggested Johnny's, a club that had beautiful exotic dancers. To hear Tommy tell it, "I was not disappointed in what I saw, and I was there several times a week. I was there so often that I became friends with Johnny, the owner. The thing is, I didn't go home every weekend, so I spent a lot of money and time at Johnny's. Johnny and I became such friends that when he got married, he asked me to be a bartender at his wedding."

Little did Tommy know that his life was about to take

a surprising turn at the wedding. Among the guests was Deborah, a petite blonde who had caught Tommy's eye at the club. She was cute, with an infectious smile that reminded him of me, as he would later tell me with a laugh—"cute, petite, and cute, ha-ha." Deborah was there too, and Johnny, knowing Tommy's interest, orchestrated their introduction. Tommy reminisced, "Johnny knew I was interested in Deborah, so as a little surprise, he introduced me to her at the wedding. What an introduction it was. Deborah and I became fast friends, and soon, we spent all our free time together."

People often asked Tommy if it ever bothered him the <u>way</u> he met Deborah "No, that never bothered me," he said with a nonchalant shrug. "And once we became a couple, she gave up that way of life. She changed her life to be with me; no telling how many men offered to take her away from that life. I just considered myself lucky with all the guys she was around and some of them were better looking than I was, but it was me who flew in and swept her away."

Tommy and Deborah shared many adventures, one of the most memorable being when she accompanied him to an air show. While flying, Deborah, ever the free spirit, was painting her fingernails and jokingly told Tommy he had better not make her spill the polish. In true Tommy Beal fashion, he performed a barrel roll without spilling a drop. "I enjoyed showing out for her, and she loved the attention," he recalled, his eyes twinkling with mischief.

In 1984, Tommy accepted a job selling planes for Mitsubishi.

He and Deborah moved to Houston, TX, and entered into a common-law marriage, beginning their lives as a married couple. Deborah also worked as a flight attendant on Tommy's plane, adding another layer to their unique relationship. Tommy seemed to have everything he wanted in his wife; she was a free spirit, flight attendant on his plane, and good-looking too. However, life had a way of complicating things. When asked what happened, Tommy said, "I just got tired of the way things were going between us. She was interested in other men, and I was partying way too much. On top of all of that, I was also homesick for Alabama. Deborah wasn't interested in leaving Houston at that point. However, after we split up, she later moved to Tennessee, moving in with her parents and sister and Todd Deborah's friend ,"

Although they were in a common-law marriage, since Deborah used his last name when they bought a house and in other legal matters in Texas, they had to get a legal divorce. The legalities were a formality, a punctuation mark at the end of a chapter in Tommy's life.

These stories painted a picture of a man searching for connection in places where connections were fleeting. Yet, they also revealed Tommy's innate ability to form genuine bonds, even in the most unexpected circumstances. As I listened to his tales, a mosaic of his life emerged—one filled with moments of joy, sorrow, and everything in between. Our paths may have diverged for forty years, but in those conversations, we found common ground, a shared history that bridged the gap of time and distance.

Tommy and I enjoy our lives as best as we can. When we got together, we talked a lot about old times, reminiscing about everything we had both been through. Tommy told me that when he saw me in the hospital, as sick as he was, he knew he wanted me back in his life, even if it meant only on the phone. We talked by phone as much as we could over the next few years, reliving old memories and realizing that our bond was still as strong as ever, even after forty years apart. Tommy seemed to just recognize something that I had long known. We had loved each other all our lives.

In 2012, Tommy faced major surgery, and I stayed with him in the hospital, determined to be by his side. The first night, he had a pain pump, and his thumb was working overtime. At one point, he looked over at me with those familiar blue eyes and said, "I love you. Will you marry me?" I naturally said yes but thought it was the drugs talking. The next morning, he asked me if I remembered what he had asked the night before. I said I did but didn't know if he had. He smiled and said that he wanted to talk to my mom about it before we went any further. Mom was, of course, delighted because she felt we should have always been together, even as kids.

As I sat by his side, holding his hand, I realized that our story was far from over. The love and friendship we had nurtured all those years ago still thrived, stronger and more resilient than ever. We had waited a lifetime to find each other again, and now, we were determined to make the most of every moment. Life had given us a second chance, and we weren't going to let it slip away. Together, we faced the future, with all its uncertainties and challenges, knowing that as long as we had each other, we could weather any storm.

We planned to get married while my brother Clark and his wife Gwen were visiting in the middle of August 2013. The anticipation was sweet, and we were filled with hope and excitement. However, tragedy struck on August 4th. I had to take my mom to the hospital. She had pneumonia and was put on a ventilator the next day. The days that followed were a blur of worry and heartache. She never recovered, and the decision was made to take her off the ventilator on the 14th. My mom was my best friend, and I was closer to her than anyone else. Over the years, she had been my rock, always offering support and an ear when I was at my lowest. Losing her was a devastating blow, and it felt like the ground had been pulled out from under me.

Yet, in the midst of my grief, Tommy was there, a steady presence, helping me navigate the stormy seas of loss. He held me when the tears wouldn't stop and listened when the words tumbled out in fits and starts. We drew strength from each other, finding solace in our shared memories and the deep connection that had stood the test of time. Our love, forged in the fires of youth and tempered by decades of separation, was a testament to the enduring power of true friendship and love.

As we moved forward, our bond grew stronger, rooted in the past but blossoming anew. We learned to cherish each moment, knowing that life's unpredictability made every second together precious. And in those moments, whether quiet and tender or filled with laughter and stories of old times, we found a love that was as timeless as the memories we shared.

Tommy took her death hard, and we talked about postponing the wedding. But in the quiet moments of reflection, we both felt Mom's presence urging us on. It was Mom's wish that we be together, so we got married on August 31, 2013. It was a bittersweet day, filled with the joy of our union and the sorrow of her absence. But we knew she was watching over us, smiling from above.

In the Spring of 2016, I retired and devoted myself to staying home and taking care of Tommy. His health had become more fragile, with limited mobility, and I wanted to be there for him, just as he had been for me. We have faced some rough medical issues since we married. Tommy continues to have TIAs, mini-strokes. He had a cholecystectomy, which was almost missed because his symptoms weren't like most people's. Luckily, his doctor recognized what it was and put him in the hospital in time. I've had knee replacement surgery, but the old ticker is holding up, a testament to the resilience of the human heart.

Tommy and I still talk all the time, our conversations a mix of the mundane and the extraordinary. Getting him to open up about his fantastic life is difficult, though. He doesn't feel he did anything special. To him, he was just doing what he loved. Flying dead bodies, presidential candidates, rock stars, and flying on 9/11 were all just part of his job. But to me, and to anyone who hears his stories, they are the stuff of legends.

Whenever he does open up, he can bring tears to your eyes with the depth of his experiences and the humility with which he recounts them. Earlier in this book, I talked about how I felt finding Tommy again. I felt special when I heard how Tommy felt. In his own words, "That day Barbara entered my hospital room, I felt both hope and despair at the same time. I was terrified to get my hopes up. Could I have my friend back? The despair? I desperately wanted her back in my life, but in the condition I was in, I felt it was unfair to ask her to be with me."

Tommy's words echoed the turmoil in my heart, a blend of yearning and fear. Yet, as we sat together, talking about the past and dreaming of the future, those fears began to dissipate. Our bond, forged in childhood and reignited in adulthood, was stronger than any doubts we had. We had been given a second chance, and we were determined to make the most of it.

"In the lifestyle I lived, I had done a lot of things that I'm sure she wouldn't like or approve of. I did have hope of getting my life back on a decent track, and maybe after that, we could be together. After all, she was my best friend growing up, someone who would listen to my dreams, walk with me in the woods, find animals, and look for angels in the big fluffy clouds. But most of all, she was always there when I needed her. Over the years, I would often reflect on the past and think of what would have, could have, should have, and what might have been, especially when I would go home and pass her old home place. My heart would ache for the old times."

Tommy's voice trembled with emotion as he shared these reflections. His eyes, once bright with the adventures of his youth, now held a depth of sorrow and wisdom. "Back in the day, I could share everything with her, but the challenge of the stroke I would have to take on by myself. At least, that is what I thought. I couldn't do anything, not even talk. Why would anyone want to be with me? Depression was a very real part of my life. It is funny, I had lived a blessed and charmed life, but the Hee-Haw despair song fit me to a 'T' at the time. 'Gloom, despair, and agony on me. Deep, dark depression, excessive misery. If it weren't for bad luck, I'd have no luck at all. Gloom, despair, and agony on me.'"

His words painted a picture of a man who had seen and done it all, yet found himself humbled and broken by the very stroke that altered the course of his life. "Yes, I was at a really low point. However, true to her form, when I was down, I would have my mom call Barbara for me. Mom would tell her how I was doing. Barbara always had a way of saying something that brought me back to reality. She would say something funny like, 'Get your butt in gear and take a walk. Stop feeling sorry for yourself.' Or she would just let me know that she was there anytime I needed her."

After that day in the hospital, laughter became a huge part of our lives. Even when I didn't see her for the next eight years, we still talked over the phone, even if it was communicating through my mom. Over the years, my progress was one step forward and two steps back. But having my best friend in my life has been a real encouragement. I once lived a bigger-than-life lifestyle. Now I am a shell of my former self. Strokes have a way of humbling a person in a way I never imagined. If someone had told me that one day, I would have to depend on someone for almost everything, I wouldn't have understood or even believed them. Yes, even today, people tell me I am special when I don't see it or feel it. In the past, I felt like I was the captain of my ship (airplane, as it were) and the master of my fate. I did what I wanted to do, testing the limits of everything. I loved seeing just how far I could push life. Flying planes, riding motorcycles, and partying with rock stars, I was just speeding through life, never taking time to slow down until the day of the stroke, when life p ushed back."

You can hear the pain in Tommy's voice as he is still dealing with a life so far removed from the one of his youth. Today, Tommy and I have a lot of people who call our lives boring. Maybe so, but we do what we want to do. We see the friends we want to see, and we go to church, which is very important to us. We both love music, so we go to as many concerts as we can. Traveling is hard on Tommy, so we stay very close to home. Tommy still sells airplanes with his friend Bill Pilker but the market hasn't been good the last couple years.

What is the Barbara and Tommy Beal love story? Although Tommy and I were apart for over forty years, neither of us ever forgot the other. We feel more connected to each other today than ever. A lot of people ask me why I would want to take on such a huge responsibility that entails taking care of someone who has had a major stroke and has so many health issues.

Our church family has been an incredible source of strength and comfort for us, especially during the most difficult times. When life seemed overwhelming, it was the unwavering support of our church that helped us find our way. They've been there for us through thick and thin, offering prayers, encouragement, and a sense of belonging that has made all the difference.

Tommy's faith, in particular, has been his anchor. It's what helped him overcome his drug dependence, a battle that tested him in ways he never imagined. During the years when we were apart, even though we couldn't be together in person, we still found a way to connect through prayer. We would talk over the phone, and as we shared our struggles and hopes, we would pray together, asking God to give Tommy the strength to fight his addiction.

I remember those conversations vividly. There was a time when Tommy was at his lowest, and the pull of addiction seemed impossible to resist. But in those moments, his faith would rise to the surface, reminding him of the person he wanted to be. We prayed for him to have the strength to overcome the temptation, to find the courage to choose a different path. And slowly, but surely, he did.

Since 2003, Tommy has been drug-free. It's a milestone that

we both cherish, a testament to his willpower and the grace of God. He knows that his recovery wasn't just about staying away from the drugs; it was about rebuilding his life on a foundation of faith and love. Tommy often says that without faith, he wouldn't have made it. And I believe him. His faith is what carried him through the darkest times and into the light.

Tommy also knew that I wouldn't have anything to do with him if he was still using. I had seen too many lives destroyed by addiction, and I couldn't bear the thought of losing him to that darkness. It wasn't an ultimatum; it was a boundary rooted in love and a desire to see him live the life he was meant to live. I wanted to be with the man I knew he could be, not the man who was held captive by his demons.

Our church family played a crucial role in his recovery. They welcomed him with open arms, offering support without judgment. They prayed for him, encouraged him, and celebrated his victories, no matter how small. Tommy found a community that believed in him, even when he struggled to believe in himself. Their love and acceptance gave him the strength to keep going, to fight for the life he wanted.

There were days when the journey seemed impossible, when the weight of his past threatened to pull him back into old habits. But in those moments, Tommy turned to his faith, to the prayers we had shared, and to the support of our church family. He learned to lean on them, to trust that he didn't have to walk this path alone. And with their help, he found the courage to move forward.

Today, we look back on those difficult times with gratitude. They were the crucible in which our faith was tested and strengthened. Our church family continues to be a source of comfort and joy for us, a reminder that we are never alone in our struggles. They have shown us the true meaning of community, of what it means to bear one another's burdens and to celebrate each other's triumphs.

Tommy's faith journey has been a powerful testament to the strength of the human spirit and the transformative power of love and faith. It's a journey we've shared together, one that has deepened our bond and renewed our hope for the future. We are grateful every day for the second chance we've been given, and we know that with God's grace and the support of our church family, we can face whatever challenges come our way.

As we continue to walk this path together, hand in hand, we do so with the knowledge that we are surrounded by love—by each other, by our church family, and by the unwavering presence of God in our lives. And in that love, we find the strength to keep moving forward, one day at a time.

Life has a way of throwing curveballs, but through it all, Tommy and I have remained steadfast. We face each challenge together, drawing strength from our love and the memories we share. Our journey has been filled with ups and downs, but it's the love and friendship that have carried us through. In each other, we have found a sanctuary, a place where we can be our true selves, unburdened by the weight of the world.

As we look back on the path that led us here, we are grateful for every twist and turn, every joy and sorrow. For it is those experiences that have shaped us and brought us to this moment. And as we move forward, hand in hand, we know that whatever the future holds, we will face it together, with the same love and resilience that has defined our journey.

Maybe it's really simple. When you have loved someone all your life, someone you can talk to, someone with whom you can share your feelings, and you share so many wonderful friends and great memories. We have been blessed. Few couples get a second chance to spend the rest of their lives loving and being loved with all their hearts. I was without him for forty-eight years, and I simply can't imagine the rest of my life without Tommy by my side.

Tommy and I love each other even more today than we did growing up. There are a lot of trials we go through, especially with his health, but he tells me every day that he loves me and can't imagine life without each other. Tommy and I wouldn't be anywhere else. I know he depends on me for his day-to-day health issues, but he doesn't abuse it. He tries his best to do what he's able to do. I think we love each other even more today than we ever did. We are still each other's best friends.

We have very few conflicts because we know what buttons to push or not push. His health is a challenge for both of us. He struggles with walking, but he manages most everything else. If we have an issue, he's quick to point out that I signed a paper agreeing to it. He has a quick wit and a great sense of humor that helps when things get tough.

Since we got back together, we have both learned the give and take in our relationship. I'm sure I give more because of his health issues, but I do know if he were able, he'd do anything in the world for me. I've learned things about him that scare me, but I trust him. I learned long ago to let the little things go, and so has Tommy. We both have moments when we are struggling, but all he has to do is hold out his hand to me, and I know everything is going to be okay.

I don't know if we would have found each other again if it hadn't been for our chance meeting while he was in the hospital. I do believe that God had and has a plan for us both. Maybe it took our years apart to appreciate each other today. I do know both of us always loved each other, even as kids. We just were not able to figure out how to be a couple. I think our long conversations while he was recovering from his stroke made us both realize that our lives have always been intertwined. He says he thought of me often, and I did him.

If I give anyone advice about marriage, it would be to make sure your faith is solid and make it a point to respect each other's views. Never go to bed without letting the other know you love them, no matter where you are. Trust each other, respect each other, and believe in each other. One thing about Tommy is that he has a great sense of humor and quick wit. He has the very best laugh; when he laughs, everyone around him laughs. When he's feeling good, it's hard to get anything over on him. This is one thing we both enjoy. I'm a prankster and love to pull pranks on him, but I have to be careful and not make him fall. Have you ever seen anyone on a walker jump when you startle them? Probably not nice, but we both laugh. I can't do it as much as we once did because his mobility is much more limited n ow.

In those moments when we sit quietly together, Tommy and I find solace in each other's company. Our love story is one of resilience and rediscovery, of finding joy in the simple moments and strength in the face of adversity. We look back on our shared past with gratitude and face the future with hope, knowing that whatever comes our way, we will face it together. Our journey has been long and winding, filled with unexpected twists and turns, but it has brought us to a place of profound love and understanding. And for that, we are truly blessed that fate finally found us.

Barb and Tommy Beal

www.ingramcontent.com/pod-product-compliance
Lightning Source LLC
Chambersburg PA
CBHW050648160426
43194CB00010B/1859